Fay Ellis

CALLED
to be
WARRIORS

"...Wherefore Take Unto You The Whole Armor Of God..." (Ephesians 6:13)

DENVER, COLORADO

This book is dedicated to the memory
of
Evangelist John David Lawrence
1929 – 1985
A WARRIOR
Called,
Chosen,
Sent,
And successful…

TABLE OF CONTENTS

PREFACE

Because of the bold onslaught of Satan against our families, churches, communities, and even our country, I felt led of God to deal with this worsening spiritual war. I have been under pressure since 1989 to pen a book dealing with the "forces of darkness," which seem to be growing more powerful: the first edition was written in 1993. Most of what I have written, God has taught me and/or I have had discussions with others in ministry. I am grateful to my son and daughter-in-law, Eric and Cynthia Butler, Kelly and Nellie Harper, John and Betty Jo Gordon, Pastor James Lee (S.C.), Charles and Michelle Garrison, and all who have shared so much with me about the end time ministry and war.

Even though these persons are deceased, I am eternally grateful to Evangelist John David Lawrence, Father Ralph N. Ellis Sr., and especially to my husband, a person of great kindness, long-suffering, and nobility for helping to bring this book to a place of understanding, commitment, and even scholarship. Bishop Norman N. Quick of New York City must be acknowledged for all the years he insisted that I write for the church. I also appreciate my oldest brother, now deceased, who encouraged me and assisted me with my first printing in 1993.

I thank my sister Joy Ellis Walker and my oldest daughter Jacqueline for their editing and valuable suggestions. I also thank my grandson, Van Don Williams II, for his desperately needed help with the computer.

I appreciate how God challenged me and instructed me through His servants. I can only give God the glory for allowing me to serve the Body of Christ in this manner.

GLOSSARY

(Names and phrases every believer should be familiar with)

Astrology: Astrology is divinational (Deut.18). It was developed by the Chaldeans of the Babylonian era to discern your future with the Zodiac.

Baby Saint: Similar to the natural explanation of an infant, the baby saint is a new Christian who needs compassionate, patient, spiritual nurturing to grow properly. That is to say, the "baby saint" will not grow or will grow deformed if not nurtured in the Word of God.

Ascended Masters: Similar to visitations by angels, whom God sends to give His saints special help or information, these are Satan's demons who bring wisdom to his servants.

Centering: Centering is used in some public schools. Centering with relaxation is believed to help the child find space to listen to the voice within. There are many ways to teach children how to become centered: "count one's breath to ten over and over," "listen for the most distant sound," "picture fluffy white clouds floating by," or "imagine a bright light filling your entire body."

Channeling: Relaxing the mind and inviting a demon or demon(s) to be your "special friend" or spirit guide. When these techniques are used in the schools, the word DEMON is NEVER USED.

Chanting: Chanting is repeating usually one word over and over to invite the presence of a demon; in Eastern transcendental meditation (TM), this is labeled a mantra.

Christian/Saint/Believer: These terms are used interchangeably to refer to any person who has accepted Christ as his/her personal Savior.

Clairvoyance: Receiving information through satanic revelation that could not have been regular knowledge to that person.

Doorways: Doorways are those areas of vulnerability to Satan's control and/or torment, particularly where there is UNFORGIVENESS.

(ESP) Extrasensory Perception: Receiving information by supernatural means, whether from demonic voices, dreams, etc.

Flesh/Sin Nature: These two terms are used interchangeably to refer to men's carnal nature and sensual appetites.

Holy Spirit/Holy Ghost: The two terms, used interchangeably, are the names of the third person in Trinity.

Idolatry: Worshiping anything more than God.

"Itching Ears": As used in II Timothy 4:3, this refers to those persons who really do not want to hear the absolute truth but rather what pleases them. Persons with itching ears regularly run to hear the latest popular prophet or preacher.

Karate/Martial Arts: Tae kwon do, karate, and even yoga are based on Eastern religious principles. As part of the training, intense meditation must take place.

Lucifer: Lucifer was Satan's angelic name before he rebelled against God.

Meditation: Cultivating a passive mind. Taught in some schools to help control children.

Medium: A medium is a person with a "familiar spirit" who can call up what is perceived to be a dead person's spirit; it is a demon that imitates the dead. The medium will go into a trance and speak with what sounds like the dead person's voice.

Mind Control: Mind control is always WITCHCRAFT. Persons who manipulate and control a person's thinking and behavior is into witchcraft, whether it is with occult practices or not. In the church this witchcraft is called a "Jezebel spirit."

Palm Readers: These persons look at various lines in a person's hand and supposedly foretell the future.

Religious Demons: These are demons that manifest themselves in church services, imitating everything that the Holy

Spirit does in the believer. These demons can speak in a multiplicity of tongues (and may be cursing God and the pastor), dance, and preach, all in what appears to be authentically of God. Note that "religious demons" are increasing in many churches.

Satanism: Satanism (like atheism) is considered a religion in America. Services are held and Satan is worshipped. Some have a cross upside down. They say the Lord's Prayer backward. At least eight times a year, they have blood sacrifices on their altar and try to have human sacrifices on Easter Eve, Christmas Eve, Thanksgiving Eve, Halloween, and on the days of the solstices (changing seasons). They also like sacrificing dogs because "dog" is "God" spelled backward. The police and law enforcement agencies rarely publicize the proliferation of human sacrifice. However, one police officer estimates it may be as high as 12,000 per year in America. Note that in communities on Long Island (New York), residents are warned to watch their pets on the nights of a full moon and on holidays. Some Satanists even imitate the Resurrection by killing a large animal and placing a small child in the dead animal in the ground and then pulling the poor child out "in the name of Satan."

Sorcery: Sorcery is the use of supernatural powers (demons) to control individuals.

Witchcraft: Usually the use of evil supernatural power to affect individual lives and behavior. In New York City there are 180 different ethnic groups; some individuals in these groups have practices that are peculiar to their culture. Many call themselves Christian: for example, Santeria from

Panama, spiritistas from Puerto Rico, Voodoo priests from Haiti, druids and Wicca witches (origins from England and Scotland), yoga from Hindu, and Buddhist influence from India and China, Juju and obeah from Jamaica, etc. So-called "black" witchcraft uses blood sacrifice, and "white" witchcraft uses mainly incantations (like Wicca witches).

Warlock or Wizard: A male witch.

INTRODUCTION

The War is on!

It is a Life-and-Death Struggle!

It is Vicious and Ugly!

The **WAR IS ON** but we are neither trained nor prepared to fight as we should be. We seem to have very little comprehension of the diverse manipulative power of Satan **RIGHT IN THE CHURCH.**

War is a state of open, armed, often prolonged conflict carried on between hostile nations, states, or parties; any condition of active antagonism and conflict. Included in this definition are the techniques or procedures of war like military science and strategy. Ignorance and unpreparedness aid the enemy and guarantee destruction by the enemy during wartime. Therefore, any person involved in any kind of war needs to be trained in techniques, tactics, and strategy as well as to be educated and informed about the enemy's ability, limitations, and power. These principles hold true in all aspects of warfare, including the **spiritual warfare** in which Satan controls a well-organized host of evil spirits.

Satan, who is always orchestrating disasters, never stops nor sleeps. He has a sophisticated hierarchy of evil demons and forces working all the time—every day, all day, and around the clock—against the will of the Father, against the Body of Christ, and against you.

"For false Christs and false prophets shall rise, and shall shew SIGNS AND WONDERS, to seduce, if it were possible, even the elect" **(Mark 13:22).**

Satan is not going to give any of us a briefing on his sophisticated plans of destruction. Only God will and does reveal Satan's evil plans to His people.

"The COMFORTER, which is THE HOLY GHOST, whom the Father will send in my name, HE SHALL TEACH YOU ALL THINGS…" **(John 14:26)** *"Howbeit when He, the SPIRIT OF TRUTH, is come, He will guide you into all truth…"* **(John 16:13)**

The Holy Ghost will work in the believer with the discerning of good and evil,[1] dreams and visions, a Word of Knowledge, prophecy, etc., but only when the believer stays in a relationship with God and **allows** the **HOLY SPIRIT TO GUIDE** and **TEACH HIM/HER.**

The Body of Christ is in trouble because we are

---

1   Discerning of spirits is one of the Gifts of the Holy Spirit (I Cor. 12.). However, every spirit-filled believer has some measure of discerning of spirits operating in their lives. Otherwise, how could the sign of casting out devils in the name of Jesus follow any believer if he could not discern evil?

underestimating and/or ignoring **the strength, the power, the organization, and the tenacity of the enemy (Satan).** To be sure, leaders do recognize the "falling away" and the "knowledge-of-God-without-the-Power" syndromes. We often discuss spiritual warfare, have so-called spiritual warfare seminars and workshops, while spiritually we are being weakened and fragmented from within and without. Unfortunately, it seems we often fail to recognize the subtle "victories" of Satan.

– We advocate prayer but rarely stay on our knees until we "pray through."

– We often preach with great brilliance and emotion, but without the anointing.

– We speak of having the victory without having temperance or patience.

– We verbally advocate love, but we usually demonstrate selfish love to those in our social network[2]; we rarely seem to really support and strengthen the elderly and feebleminded among us.

It appears that all too often we have not distinguished between church work and "Kingdom work," nor taken time to explain and understand the WORKS that God accepts.

"For other foundation can no man lay that is laid, which is Jesus. Now if any man build upon this

---

2   Read James 2:1-9.

foundation gold, silver, precious stones, wood, hay, stubble; every man's work shall be made manifest: for the day shall declare it, because it shall be revealed by fire; and the fire shall try every man's work of what sort it is." (I Cor. 3:11-13)

"Church work" as opposed to "Kingdom work" is here defined as all those activities and functions, including fund-raising, that maintain, improve, and perpetuate the existing building(s), clubs, auxiliaries, and financial income of the church. Church work is not mutually exclusive from Kingdom work. However, there should be a balance, with Kingdom work being the central focus. Kingdom work is therefore defined as any and all of the labor for God that could stand being tried in the fire: **saving and delivering souls, healing sick bodies, travailing prayer for families and communities, mending broken homes, rescuing and training children, developing disciples and warriors for God, and supporting home and foreign missions.**

Nothing is wrong with having a wide range of ministries and raising money for the ministry. Unfortunately, the "deceiver" has managed to involve too many spiritual leaders in fund-raising, church administration, developing programs, and erecting buildings that should be secondary to "the works that can be tried in the fire."

Lulling leaders and members into a state of spiritual complacency by implementing **more and more church services, meetings, and programs in church buildings with church folk** is a deceptive strategy of Satan for the subtle weakening of the Power of God operating in the Body of Christ. **We are at WAR!!!**

- The laity as well as clergy are contracting and dying of AIDS (in all denominations) because of sexual preference and orientation.

- The frequency and rate of divorce is escalating among church members at the same rate as non-church members, over 60 percent.

- Too many of our unmarried young people are sexually active; young ladies in the church are having abortions and/or babies out of wedlock. Similarly, we are losing our young men to drugs, prison, and illegal activities, and many to violent deaths.

- It appears that no longer is it a general practice that you must be "born again" to become an active church member while holding administrative and leadership positions. Often, churches with vibrant, sophisticated programs and rapid church growth have embezzlers on the trustee board, homosexuals running the music department, hostile persons running the usher board, and some church officials who appear to be more concerned about their personal appearance than souls, etc.

- Church leaders and laity alike have pledged to secret societies like the Masons and the Eastern Star.[3]

---

3   *Masonry, Beyond the Light*, by William Schnoebelen (Chick Publications, 1991), does an excellent job dealing with occult/satanic

Every Christian must understand that **as soon as he/she accepts the Lord, he/she is engaged in spiritual warfare!!!** This book, then, is written not as a complete rendition of Satan's warfare, but as a teaching tool to assist believers in better understanding Satan's warfare against the church and every born-again individual. In addition, this book deals with information on how to better RECOGNIZE Satan's strategies, how to RESIST Satan, and how to BIND, REBUKE, AND CAST THE DEVIL[4] OUT.

Then the serious discussion will deal with Satan's well-organized kingdom and how he uses it against the Body of Christ and individual Christians. The chapters dealing with Satan are specifically designed to give insight into the danger of **spiritual slothfulness** and **spiritual ignorance.**

Therefore, there will be an exploration of man's **sin nature/ the flesh** (the natural tendency to be selfish, self-centered, and self-serving), but more specifically, how the **sin nature** works against the Christian's sanctification. Since where **the flesh** is ruling, the Holy Spirit will not, there is an in-depth discussion on how the flesh (working with inherited gifts, acquired skills, inherited positions, traditions of men) excludes God and includes Satan in church work.

The last chapters will discuss tactics and strategy, like battle plans of a real war. There will be discussion on the tools, preparation, and techniques of war.

The basics of the Christian experience have been dealt with

---

nature and the origins of these organizations.

4   The names "Satan" and "the devil" are used interchangeably.

in my book entitled **CALLED TO BE S**AINTS**; this book, **CALLED TO BE WARRIORS,** is a sequel.

Being a WARRIOR is not an option; it is a mandate by God!

> *"Fear thou not for I am with thee: be not dismayed; for I AM THY GOD: I will strengthen thee; yea I will help thee; Yea, I WILL UPHOLD THEE with the right hand of my righteousness."* (Isaiah 41:10)

THE FATHER, THE SON, AND THE HOLY GHOST

GOD, THE FATHER

It would be a mistake to attempt an explanation and/or definition of God. It is understood that the plural form of God, *ELOHIM*, is used throughout the Bible, starting in Genesis, the first chapter, and this indicates the Father, Son, and the Holy Spirit. Jesus spoke throughout the Gospels (Matthew, Mark, Luke, and John) and often said "the Father and I are one." Further, we do know to pray to the Father in the Name of Jesus.

However, if anyone could fully explain God, His power and character, then God would not be God. There is no standard or criterion higher than God Himself; consequently, we have no basis to fully explain God. Notice how Solomon expressed God's awesome power and creative ability: *"As thou knowest not what is the way of the spirit (wind), nor how the bones do grow in the womb of her that is with child: even so thou **knowest not the works of God who maketh all"** (Eccl. 11:5). God Himself is His own standard.

Further, as we read and understand the Word of God, we become fully aware that God is not confined to, or limited by, time. **God created time.** Therefore, He is, for earth and man, the beginning and end (Alpha and Omega), in spite of the fact that His existence goes from everlasting to everlasting, and His presence is everywhere all at the same time (Psalm 139:2-12).

> *"Then the Lord answered Job out of the WHIRLWIND, and said... Where was thou when I laid the foundations of the earth? Declare if thou hast understanding... Who hath laid the measures thereof, if thou knowest? ...Whereupon are the foundations thereof fastened?...Or who shut up the sea with doors, when it brake forth, as if it had issued out of the womb? Has thou entered into the treasures of the snow? Or has thou seen the treasures of the hail? Canst thou lift up thy voice to the clouds, that abundance of waters may cover thee? Canst thou send lightnings, that they may go, and say unto thee, here we are?"* **(Job 38: 1, 4-6, 8, 22, 34, 35).**

The awesomeness of God's power, wisdom, and might, as indicated in the above scriptures, may be beyond our total comprehension. **Each of us MUST** believe that **GOD IS, AND THAT HE IS A REWARDER OF** each person who **DILIGENTLY** seeks Him (Heb. 11:6). God's JUSTICE, His absolute fairness, His total equity, and His eternal equality, in regard to the self-determining capacity of man, Satan, and angels need to be highlighted. God freely gave man, Lucifer (Satan), and all the angels/ freedom to LOVE HIM and OBEY HIM or not to LOVE HIM and OBEY HIM.

Today the word "justice" often refers to punishment. However, GOD'S **JUSTICE** refers to God's fairness and most simply means that God allows man,[5] angels,[6] and Satan "the right of free choice." Understand that God in His fairness gave Lucifer **the free choice to rebel**. It would follow, then, that God, who is absolutely just and fair, **did not take free choice and decision-making power from Lucifer when he became Satan, who continues to be totally evil**.

Similarly, the first man, Adam, had free choice to eat or not to eat of the *forbidden fruit* (Gen. 2:17). Man has been given a will that God will not violate. Yet God in His consummate love for man knew man would fail and was prepared to give his Son to reconcile all men back to Himself. As Revelations 13:8 clearly states, that He, Jesus, was the Lamb slain before the foundation of the World.

JESUS, THE SON OF GOD

"Looking unto Jesus the author and finisher of our faith; who for the joy that was set before him endured the cross, despising the shame, and is set down at the right hand of the throne of God. For consider him that endured such contradiction against himself, lest ye be wearied and faint in your minds." **(Hebrews 12:2, 3)**

---

5   In many of the New Testament scriptures, the use of *let* means *you allow.* In other words, USE YOUR WILL. (Consider II Cor.7:1; Phil.2:5; Col.3:16.)
6   Jude 6.

Jesus was in the beginning of creation as indicated in Genesis 1:26, *"LET US make man..."* Further, in all of the creation account in Genesis, the Hebrew word for God is used in its plural form—*ELOHIM*. Even after The Fall, God still wanted man to be in a relationship with Him. Therefore, Jesus' sacrificial death was THE PLAN OF REDEMPTION. Genesis 3:15 was the first prophetic scripture concerning Jesus' sacrificial death, making provision for man to be reconciled back to God.[7]

> *"And he is before all things and by him all things consist. And he is the head of the body, the church: who was in the beginning, the firstborn from the dead; that in all things he might have the preeminence... And having made peace through the blood of HIS CROSS, by him to reconcile all things unto himself..."* **(Col. 1:17, 18, 20)**

A human body was prepared for Jesus (Hebrews 10:5) so that as the Captain of our Salvation (Hebrews 2:10; 5:8, 9), He would be the Perfect Example. Knowing the terrible suffering to come, He chose to demonstrate by example that absolute obedience and total love for God was absolutely possible. He stated concerning his crucifixion, *"No man taketh it from me* (His Life)*, but I lay it down of myself. I have power to lay it down and I have power to take it again..."* (John 10:18). Jesus, knowing the Love of God for man, was pleased to suffer in order to provide a way for man to be reconciled back to God.

---

7   In Gen. 3:15 *"Thou shall bruise his heel"* refers to Satan's future challenge to Jesus during his life on earth. *"It shalt bruise thy head"* foreshadows Satan's defeat at the resurrection.

"For both HE THAT SANCTIFIETH and THEY WHO ARE SANCTIFIED are all of one: for which cause HE IS NOT ASHAMED TO CALL THEM BRETHREN." (Hebrews 2:11)

The job of every individual is simple; to believe and receive the Work of Calvary and the Blood of the Cross. The believer then steps into a realm of almost limitless power: *"But as many as received him, to them gave He Power to become sons of God, even to them that believe on his name"* (John 1:12). The believer is adopted into the Family of God and gains privileges and responsibilities as a child of God: *"And if children, then heirs; HEIRS OF GOD, and JOINT-HEIRS with Christ..."* (Romans 8:17).

As sons and daughters of God, ALL BELIEVERS have immediate access to the throne of God to find help in the time of need (Hebrews 4:14-16), and are guided and led by THE SPIRIT OF GOD as well (Romans 8:14). Furthermore, the Gospel of John identifies man's COMPLETENESS, WHOLENESS, and SAFETY in JESUS.

"I AM the Bread of LIFE." (John 6:35)

The Word states that He satisfies that spiritual hunger because *"Blessed are they which do HUNGER and thirst after righteousness; for they SHALL BE FILLED"* (Matt. 5:6).[8]

"I AM the LIGHT of the World." (John 8:12)

---

8   Compare Psalm 107:9.

Every believer is complete in Him because *"...God, who commanded the LIGHT to shine out of darkness, hath shined in our hearts..."* (II Cor. 4:6) and freed us from darkness (Col. 1:13; Psalm 119:105).

"I AM The DOOR of the Sheep." (John 10:7)

The metaphor "sheep" infers that only the obedient can go through this **DOOR,** which gives access to the Father (John 14:6; Eph. 2:18). Christ, as the **DOOR,** gives protection (Psalm 23) and spiritual security as long as the sheep remain obedient (John 10:28, 29).

"I AM the Resurrection and the LIFE." (John 11:25)

Whoever believes and receives Jesus has SPIRITUAL LIFE, which physical death cannot end. If Jesus **IS LIFE,** He can restore life. In two respects He is the **RESURRECTION.** First, Christians are no longer DEAD IN THEIR TRESPASSES AND SINS, and secondly, ALL WHO DIE IN CHRIST SHALL RISE AGAIN (I Thess. 4:15, 16).

"I AM your MASTER and LORD." (John 13:13)

Jesus is the believer's **MASTER** (*didaskalos,* meaning "teacher") in the sense of guiding and instructing. In addition, **LORD** (*kurios*) signifies authority in the sense of ownership. When the believer willingly testifies *"I am no longer my own,"* he/she means **Jesus is Lord of my life, my substance, my time, and my finance—my everything!**

"I AM the WAY, the TRUTH, and the LIFE." (John 14:6)

Jesus as **THE WAY** is the only way to the Father. Jesus as **THE TRUTH** is the only way to know and receive the promises of God. Jesus as **THE LIFE** is that part of the Savior that allows the believer to have His Spirit and have eternal life immediately. God loved the world so much, **He** gave His only Son (John 3:16); **His Son** gave His Life (John 10:18) in order to become the acceptable sacrifice for our sins (I John 2:2). Jesus, having paid the Perfect Price, gives an open invitation to everyone everywhere.

> *"Come unto me, ALL ye that labor and are heavy laden, and I will give you rest. Take my yoke upon you, and LEARN of me; for I am meek and lowly in heat: and ye SHALL find rest for your souls. For my yoke is EASY and my burden is LIGHT."* (Matt. 11:28-30)

> *"All that the Father giveth to me shall come to me; and him that cometh to me I will in no wise cast out."* (John 6:37)

Furthermore, Jesus baptizes and fills all believers with **The Holy Spirit** and will continue to abide within all who live in obedience to the Word of God. *"And we are his witnesses of these things; and so is also the Holy Ghost, who God HATH GIVEN TO THEM THAT OBEY HIM."* (Acts 5:32)

THE HOLY SPIRIT/THE HOLY GHOST

The Holy Spirit (Holy Ghost) was in the beginning with **the Father and the Son** at work creating the universe (Psalm

104:30). Like **the Father and the Son,**

- **He** is Omnipresent—everywhere (Psalm 139:7);

- **He** is Omniscient—all-knowing (II Cor. 2:10-11);

- **He** is Eternal (Hebrews 9:14);

- **He** is equal with **the Father** and **the Son** (Matt.18:19-20);

- **He** is called God (Acts 5:3, 4).

In the Old Testament, **the Holy Spirit** worked for man and with man by descending on man for specific tasks: **He** rested on Moses to lead the children of Israel (Numbers 11:17); **the Holy Spirit** descended on Othneil to judge Israel (Judges 3:10); **He** rested on Gideon to defeat the Midianites and the Amalekites (Judges 6:34); **the Spirit of the Lord** gave Samson superhuman strength at special times (Judges 14:6,19); **the Holy Spirit** even came upon Saul and caused him to prophesy (I Sam. 10:10); **the Spirit of God** came upon Zachariah to warn Israel about their transgression (II Chron. 24:20). Throughout the Old Testament there are many other incidents where **the Spirit of the Lord (Holy Ghost)** rested on and/or worked through individuals for very specific tasks and callings.

However, under this "'Dispensation of Grace," **the Holy Spirit** abides or dwells in the baptized believer and will work the will of **the Father and the Son** by guiding, instructing, and teaching individuals on a personal level, as well as equipping each one to defeat the devil.

"And I (Jesus) will pray the Father, and he shall give you another Comforter (the Holy Spirit), that he may ABIDE WITH YOU FOREVER." (John 14:16)

"Now we have received, not the spirit of the world, but the SPIRIT WHICH IS OF GOD; that we might know the things that are freely given us of God." (I Cor. 2:12)

Every Spirit-filled believer who remains saved and continues to sanctify everything (including sinful thoughts) out of their lives can make it in God. It is a process. Therefore, *"As many as are led by the Spirit of God, they are the sons of God"* (Romans 8:14).

Jesus knows of Satan's malicious hatred for all people. Even though Satan is the "prince of this world," "the prince of the powers of the air," "the ruler of darkness," etc., having the **POWER OF GOD, THE HOLY GHOST** is more than adequate to keep the enemy defeated. Therefore, Jesus instructed BELIEVERS to *OCCUPY* until He, the Lord, returns (Luke 19:13). He emphatically stated:

"Behold I give unto you POWER to TREAD on serpents and scorpions, and over all the power of the enemy and nothing shall by any means hurt you." (Luke 10:19)

"YE ARE OF GOD, little children, and have

*OVERCOME them: because GREATER IS HE
THAT IS IN YOU than he that is in the world."* (I
John 4:4)

*"...BUT THE PEOPLE THAT DO KNOW THEIR
GOD SHALL BE STRONG, AND DO EXPLOITS."*
(Dan. 11:32)

The Holy Spirit is the executive arm of the Godhead working the Will of the Father and the Son in the earth through every **SPIRIT-FILLED BELIEVER.**

Becoming a WARRIOR is not an option.

It is a MANDATE.

"I can do all things through Christ, which strengtheneth me." (Phil.4:13)

SATAN

HIS ORIGIN

Satan had a GLORIOUS beginning: **he was not the devil in the beginning.** God created him as a magnificent, gifted archangel (Seraphim) with free choice and placed him right in the Holy Mountain of God. He was **CREATED BY GOD AS LUCIFER!!!**

"For by him (God) *were all things created, that are in heaven, and that are in earth, visible and invisible, whether they be thrones, or dominions, or principalities, or powers; all things were CREATED BY HIM AND FOR HIM…"* (Colossians 1:16)

Because of his absolute beauty and wisdom (Ezekiel 28:12, 13), Lucifer was aware of his own uniqueness and power. Since Lucifer was created a perfect being **WITH FREE CHOICE,** his wisdom, beauty, and power seduced him into forgetting that **he was created by God to serve and obey God.**

"Thou art the anointed cherub that covereth; and I

have set thee so: thou wast upon the holy mountain of God; thou hast walked up and down in the midst of the stones of fire. Thou wast perfect in all thy ways from the day that thou wast created, till iniquity was found in thee... Thine heart was lifted up because of thy beauty, thou hast CORRUPTED thy wisdom by reason of thy brightness: I will cast thee to the ground." (Ezekiel 28:14, 15, 17)

Lucifer's rebellion occurred at an unknown period in the timeless past; no one can determine when it occurred. Nevertheless, after creation Lucifer (Satan) appeared in the Garden of Eden as a wily, evil, but beautiful serpent (Gen. 3:1).

HIS FALL AND HIS TRANSFORMATION

Lucifer's name meant **"Day-Star," "Son of the Morning,"** and **"the Light-bearer."** However, he became lifted up and decided...

"I WILL ascend into heaven,

I WILL exalt my throne above the stars of God:

I WILL sit also upon the mount of the congregation, in the sides of the north:

I WILL ascend above the heights of the clouds;

I WILL be like THE MOST HIGH. " (Is.14:13, 14)[9]

The Lord, Lucifer's creator, said, **"How art thou fallen from heaven, O Lucifer, son of the morning!"**(Is. 14:12). Lucifer, previously known as "the Light-bearer," became THE PRINCE OF DARKNESS. Because he chose to rebel against God, he was cast out of heaven. But he retained his wisdom, his beauty, and his musical ability; only now he perverts and corrupts all that was given to him by God. For example, because he was the **"Day Star" (the Light-bearer)**, Satan is able to transform himself into an evil "angel of light" (to deceive men), even though all "sinful darkness" originates from Satan.

Satan is not king, but he is the ruler of everyone who is not in a covenant relationship with God. Satan's original sins were **pride, selfishness, and rebellion.** This world's systems, ideologies, governments, wars, and philosophies evolve out of the same original sin complex—**PRIDE, SELFISHNESS,**

---

9   Without splitting theological hairs, Ezekiel 28:12-19 and Isaiah 14:4-21 need to be explained in terms of their multiple or at least dual prophetic messages. First of all the Prince of Tyre and the Prince of Persia, wicked kings, were being given messages from God. In spite of the fact that there is no direct mention of Satan in either passage, Satan is yet the subject also. Notice that some of the phrases could not be addressed to any mortal: "*You had the seal of perfection..., You were in Eden...; you were on the holy mountain of God...; you were blameless in your ways from the day you were created, until unrighteousness was found in thee...*" *(Ezekiel 28 12-15).* Further it should be obvious to any serious student of the Bible that there is frequently double meaning and fulfillment of biblical prophecy. For example, a cursory study of the Messianic Psalms would demonstrate this. In Psalm 22 David's experience and prayer were mixed with prophecies concerning the Lord's death.

AND REBELLION. All around us, and on a daily basis, we observe manifestations of **greed for power and money, perverted and polluted sex, increasing individual violence perpetrated on the innocent, including sexual slavery, and epidemic wars and political coups that are all outgrowths of the basic nature of the "prince of this world."**

Satan has many names, like the "accuser," "the father of lies," and "Beelzebub," and understanding the names of Satan will give insight to his ugly, evil nature.[10]

THE CHARACTERISTICS OF CORRUPTION

In addition to corrupting the gifts God created in him, Lucifer **WILLFULLY** chose evil. All of the evil characteristics Satan willfully adopted operate in man's sin nature.

Satan's Pride

> *"Thine heart was lifted up because of thy beauty..."* **(Ezekiel 28:17)**[11]

The pride of Lucifer was THE BEGINNING OF SORROW. God told Lucifer, *"Your heart became PROUD on account of your beauty..."* Remember out of the heart are the issues of life (Prov. 4:23), and whatever is stored in there will come out.

---

10 See Appendix I, which explains his names vis-a-vis his nature.
11 God is speaking to Satan in the text.

"For out of the abundance of the heart the mouth speaketh. A good man out of the good treasure of his heart bringeth forth good things; and an evil man out of the evil treasure bringeth forth evil things." (Matt. 12:34, 35)

Pride was the first sin of the mind and spirit. Pride is arrogance, haughtiness, and presumptuousness. It gives self all the credit for the blessings of God, whether it is financial success, good health, good looks, or great talent. This is not the pride that one has about good job performance or excellent productivity. This pride is an excessively high opinion of oneself—arrogance and conceit. For this cause the Word states, *"Pride goeth before destruction..."* (Prov. 16:18).

The heart is deceitful above all things and desperately wicked... I the Lord search the heart and examine the mind to reward a man according to his conduct, according to what his deeds deserve." (Jer. 17:9, 10)

Your **heart can lie to you.** Didn't Lucifer become so impressed with his beauty and abilities that he thought he could take over God's throne? That's how he became "*a liar from the beginning, the father of all lies*" (John 8:44). Having the sin nature of Satan (Lucifer), man is subject to think more highly of himself than he ought (Romans 12:3). Consequently, man has the predisposition for pride and self-centeredness residing in his heart.

SATAN'S HUNGER FOR POWER

It was inevitable, if pride and self-deception were in Lucifer, that he **would** become hungry for God's power. He wanted to have a throne above God's throne and thought he could supplant the Godhead. *"He said I will raise my throne above the stars of God" (Isaiah 14:13).* And, since Satan is now the "prince of this world," the same spirit operates in men. Fascinating how the extremely rich are never satisfied with all money they could never spend. Pride expands to greed for power over other businesses and then political power over nations. This **pride** and **hunger for power** has been and still is the source of international conflict all over the world, whether in Alexander of Macedon, the Caesars of Ancient Rome, Napoleon of France, Hitler of Germany, etc.

Germaine to this book, however, is how this characteristic operates within the Body of Christ. In many churches, individuals will make decisions and act in ways perceived to be career advancement strategies. If they are preachers, their gospel may be compromised, from **convicting** to **entertaining.** Or, males and females become like page boys/girls, lackeys, valets, butlers, and maids because they desire to garner favor. **Hunger for power** because of pride prefaces other sins.

SATAN'S REBELLION

Lucifer's next step in his downfall was his rebellion ADDED to his enormous dose of PRIDE. In Isaiah 14:13, 14 Lucifer (Satan) boldly stipulates his rebellion with six "I WILLs," including *"I will raise my throne above the stars of God."*

In the first place, he presumptuously decided he had a throne. In the second place all that he was and that he was given charge of was given to him by God. **Rebellion is presumptuous use of authority and power that does not belong to a person.** For example, when King Saul took priestly authority and offered sacrifices, and disobeyed the precise commandments of God, he was rebelling against the Will of God and was cut off from his kingly and spiritual heritage.

"For rebellion is as the sin of witchcraft, and stubbornness is as iniquity and idolatry. Because thou hast rejected the Word of the Lord, the Lord has rejected thee from being king." (I Sam. 15:23, 34)

Rebellion is UGLY. Children and teenagers who rebel against parents are rebelling against God's moral and spiritual order. They are, without realizing it, in mortal danger. The first commandment with promise is to *"...honor thy father and mother that THY DAYS MAY BE LONG..."* (Exo. 20:12).

Rebellion can be COSTLY. For example, insubordination in the workplace results in job termination.

Rebellion is **physically and spiritually dangerous** in the church (whether it is blatant disobedience, slothfulness, and/or sowing discord).[12] Naturally, Satan will take advantage slowly and subtly until he has managed to defile that member in rebellion and those around him/her.

---

12 Read Proverbs 6:16,19.

EXAMPLE

One woman with a very strong will and personality became almost like a witch with the negative influence she wielded against the ministry of the church and the pastor and his wife. Seemingly because she could not carve out a sphere of power and influence in the church, she began to be used by Satan (perhaps without even realizing it). This started innocently enough with dinners at her house after service on Sundays where much malicious gossip took place concerning the pastor and his wife.

She then moved her membership; next her son, who was a minister, moved to the same church. She continued to manipulate families of her former church with a lot of negative talk. Another family (under her influence) became weaker and weaker in the faith until they backslid and stopped attending church. At least two other families (under her subtle but malicious influence) left the church. Satan has used her well; her son, after ten or more years of preaching, is still just a minister and not yet ordained. One family who left has had numerous discipline problems with all their children; the other family's children have gotten into problems and have become separated from family and church. Her situation is worst of all—a cancer victim **of the mouth.**

NO ONE WINS IN REBELLION!

SATAN'S REJECTION CAUSED HIS RAGE, BITTERNESS, ANGER, MALICE

Rejection follows rebellion. When Satan rebelled, he was thrown out of heaven—**REJECTED.**[13] God told Satan he would be thrown out of heaven (Isaiah 14:15). Satan became so angry, he was determined to cause every man, woman, boy, and girl to experience **REJECTION** and hell. Rejection manifests itself in many ways and takes many forms.

- A father or mother abandoning the family is **REJECTION.**

- Sexual abuse and misuse of any kind is **REJECTION.**

- Being criticized more than being encouraged is **REJECTION.**

- Being disciplined more than being loved is **REJECTION.**

- Discrimination, racism, and sexism are all types of **REJECTION.**

Resentment, bitterness, inferiority, rage, wrath, and maybe even murder and/or suicide may follow and/or accompany rejection.

Satan is brilliant and competent. With his evil he can master any carnal Christian and any prayerless church. The Bible does not, in general, give extensive detail on Satan's

---

13   Read *Rejection, The Ruling Spirit*, by Fay Ellis Butler.

operations and methods, because Satan, first of all, imitates God, and secondly, he can change strategies against any group or person as convenient. It should not be too difficult to understand why gifts—the gifts of prophecy, discerning of spirits, the word of knowledge, etc.—are given, for the Body of Christ is to discern evil and cry out against evil as well as encourage believers.

Becoming a WARRIOR is not an option.

It is a MANDATE.

"Seek ye the Lord, while he may be found, call ye upon him while he is near." (Isaiah 55:6)

UNDERSTANDING SATAN AND THE UNSEEN WAR

"For we wrestle not against flesh and blood, but against principalities, against powers, against rulers of the darkness of this world, against spiritual wickedness in high places." (Eph. 6:12)

Satan was in the holy mountain of God and was created by God as an archangel. He was full of wisdom, and was given the name Lucifer. As Lucifer, a powerful archangel, he was fully aware of God's organization and hierarchy. To understand how he imitates, consider God's hierarchy:

THE FATHER, THE SON, AND THE HOLY GHOST

ARCHANGELS: GABRIEL, MICHAEL, ETC.

CHERUBIMS AND SERAPHIMS

OTHER WARRING ANGELS

MESSENGER ANGELS

MINISTERING ANGELS

ANGELS THAT CAMP ABOUT BELIEVERS

APOSTLES, PROPHETS, EVANGELISTS, PASTORS,

AND

TEACHERS

ALL BELIEVERS

SATAN'S HIERARCHY OF EVIL

With all his wisdom, Satan is not capable of being original. He even has a TRINITY of evil—**the beast, the false prophet, and the antichrist.** Obviously, being located *upon the holy mountain of God* (prior to being cast out of heaven), Satan, then known as Lucifer, had firsthand knowledge of the plans of God and therefore understands God's hierarchy and organization well enough to imitate God. **However, Satan, unlike God, is not everywhere all at the same time.** He has innumerable hosts of demons and powers that he rules; they are regimented to take orders from him, carry out the orders, and report back to him. Notice his organization:

Satan

His "princes" ruling vast territories and nations

Powers

"Rulers of Darkness" of this world

Spiritual wickedness in high places (the heavenlies)

"Ruling spirits" over communities

"Ruling spirits in families" (generational curses)

Demons (familiar spirits) that "follow" individuals

**Witches, Wizards, Sorcerers,
Occult workers of every type**

**Various demons of insanity, depression,
oppression, violence, etc.**

The Unsaved

Satan has a highly sophisticated hierarchy of devils with different functions and gradations of power. As viewed by the author, each category of evil as listed in Ephesians 6:12 represents a separate and distinct order of evil with its own hierarchy. The "ruling spirits" in each category report directly to Satan; the less powerful demons in every chain of command answer to those more powerful demons above them in Satan's well-organized hierarchy. On every level Satan's orders and operations are explicit and deadly. Just consider some of the specifics from the hierarchy listed above.

Familiar Spirits

There are legions of demons with special assignments: **"familiar spirits."** Since Satan attempts to imitate everything that God does—***"the angel of the Lord encampeth about them that fear him and delivereth them"* (Psalm 34:7)**—Satan has a demon, **a familiar spirit,** following each person all of his/her life. He knows the person's voice, what the person likes and dislikes. Even though it is true that Satan cannot read a person's mind, he knows how the individual thinks (based on past behavior and speech). Having had a spirit assigned to a person, Satan will attempt to inject thoughts into the mind (based on observations of their past behavior) while the person assumes it is their thoughts. **BUT SATAN KNOWS YOU, AND THE FAMILIAR SPIRIT HAS ALWAYS BEEN AROUND YOU.**

If you know Satan is real, you should also know that his hierarchy of evil is VERY REAL AND VERY VALUABLE TO HIM, especially **familiar spirits.**[14]

Satan's Special Servants

There are those believers in the Body of Christ who are available to God as Apostles, Evangelists, Prophets, Pastors, and Teachers. Again, Satan imitates the plan of God to bring man back to Himself. Satan has individuals who are sent forth with special powers that manipulate the mind and keep men bound in their **sin nature.** Some of these are witches, sorcerers, wizards, warlocks, diviners (readers of tea leaves and cards), palm readers, psychics, as well as false prophets. These individuals, used with satanic gifts, are like the prophets and preachers of the church. Therefore, witches, sorcerers, palm readers, etc. have believers and followers. Or, although many do not subscribe to the occult, they are nevertheless fearful.

---

14 Mediums "calling up" the dead during séances are performing "a lying wonder"; they use familiar spirits of the deceased. The voice and sometimes the apparition seem to be that of the deceased; it is a familiar spirit.

The Unsaved

An unsaved person is a servant of sin and Satan; Satan can therefore (because of innate selfishness and pride) keep sinners obeying him without realizing it.

"Don't you know that to whom ye yield yourselves servants to obey, his servants ye are to whom ye obey; whether of sin unto death, or of obedience unto righteousness." (Romans 6:16)

Warriors can fight **ONLY if they know WHO the enemy is, his strengths, his weaknesses, WHERE he is, WHAT his plans and implementation strategies are**. That's why the people of God must be filled with the Holy Spirit to adequately discern the evil around them. All Christians must understand that Satan plans to take as many persons as possible (from every nation, culture, social status, **and church)** to hell (the lake of fire) with him (Rev. 20:10). Most Christians understand that Satan is a powerful fallen archangel, but it appears that not enough individuals in the **BODY OF CHRIST** understand his methods, techniques, or tools.

Believers must know that Satan has power, but he is not all powerful, and that his power in the earth continues to **be limited by Spirit-filled believers**.

EXPLANATIONS OF SATAN'S HIERARCHY

Principalities or Territorial Rulers

These are the powerful princes in Satan's kingdom who have been assigned authority in particular nations and groups. Biblically, this is documented in the account of Daniel's prayer, which was hindered twenty-one days by the "prince of Persia," a powerful demon in charge of Persia (Daniel 10). Notice that one of heaven's great archangels, Michael, had to be dispatched to deal with this powerful demon (prince), and it took twenty-one days of fighting to defeat this powerful demon in charge of orchestrating evil in the Empire of Persia.

Certainly, in our time, it should not be too difficult to recognize the great ruling power of these "demonic princes" assigned to nations. After its defeat in World War I, with economic depression following and long known to be a warlike nation, Germany became filled with bitterness and hatred.[15] Germany became open to the absolute rule of the violent "prince" (ruling demon) assigned to it. Subsequently, a vessel, who was full of **hatred, bitterness, rejection, and insanity,** was prepared for this ruling demon over Germany—that vessel was Hitler.

Or consider the United States of America, which is dominated,

---

15 Read *The Rise and Fall of the Third Reich* by Shirer. One very immediately obvious fact revealed in this book is that Hitler's evil but powerful charisma was supernatural and that all the brilliant but amoral and evil men around him (Goebbels, Himmler, and Goering) had their evil brilliance magnified by Satan.

manipulated, and controlled by the ruling demonic "**prince of materialism**" or more simply put, **greed and money.** Even though the Puritans came to America seeking religious freedom, most colonizing nations like England and Spain (Ponce de Leon and others) came looking for gold, spices, and territory; in other words, wealth and power. These powerful colonializing nations created the ideal opening for a ruling demonic **prince of materialism** to rule in the unseen realm over America. This same ruling **prince** has worked relentlessly toward bringing a gradual but pernicious degradation and deterioration of America's moral, social, and political life because of greed. This demon manifests itself mainly in the drive of people for material things, often at any cost, at every social, political, and economic stratum because of the **love of money.**

One only has to look at the decade of the eighties and consider these new, but much worse Wall Street robber barons and bank thieves in the new millennium. These robber barons (under the watchful eye of the **prince of materialism**) created worthless stock and sold it to innocent people hungry to make more money: This was repeated in the first decade of the new millennium. Others created business intrigues and took over major corporations with job and financial losses to more innocent people. Worse yet was the Savings and Loan scandals in which friends and relatives of bank officers borrowed millions of dollars without any intention of paying it back, causing many innocent people to lose their investments and life savings. This unconscionable action by a few that harmed many was…

ALL FOR MONEY.

Remember, a nation whose trust is supposed to be in God "won the west" by confiscating land, breaking treaties, and almost destroying indigenous cultures of Native Americans. Further, the actions of highly esteemed traders and businessmen of this country (as well as European nations) were a major contributing factor in causing the great societal and political disorganization on the continent of Africa[16] as well as almost culturally and psychologically destroying a whole race of people of color with the infamous Transatlantic Slave Trade.

ALL FOR MONEY.

Right now in the United States of America, billion-dollar businesses proliferate (under the watchful eye of the "**prince of America**") that are amoral, immoral, and criminal; insider trading, illegal drugs, prostitution, including child prostitution, pornography, gambling of every type, a polluted entertainment media, etc.

ALL FOR MONEY.

"But they that will be rich fall into temptation and a snare, and into many foolish and hurtful lusts, which drown men in destruction and perdition. For the LOVE OF MONEY IS THE ROOT OF ALL EVIL; which while some coveted after, they have erred from the faith, and pierced themselves

---

16   The slave trade was an important enabling factor for European colonialism. Read *How Colonialism Underdeveloped Africa*, by Walter Rodney.

through with many sorrows." **(I Tim. 6:9, 10)**

Christians must become aware of the pervasive influence of a powerful ruling spirit in America because Christians, too, can be manipulated by **the love of money.**

Ruling Spirits Over Communities

In his organization of evil, Satan also has ruling demons (spirits) over communities that are subject to or work with the ruling demon over the nation or region. This is not unlike kings and monarchs in countries who have lesser royalty, nobles, and subjects assigned different tasks.

In some communities it is very obvious that an evil spirit is ruling. For example, the greed for land in America perpetrated a great injustice on the Native Americans. These populations, who could no longer range the plains and hunt, had everything dear to their culture violated and/or destroyed; rejection, hopelessness, and rage settled in on many noble Native American populations. The **ruling spirit** that settled over so many of these Native American communities is **rejection (with hopelessness)** of which **alcoholism** and family violence are byproducts. Yes, many things can be explained historically, but the unseen causes, the **ruling spirits** over communities, must be acknowledged.

In the East New York community of Brooklyn, New York, Satan has gradually sent enough poverty, unemployment, despair, and high-rise low-income housing that the **ruling spirits** of **substance abuse and violence** have given this community in the nineties the highest murder rate in the city (and the lowest reading scores).

Ruling Spirits in Families

A **ruling spirit** is a demon spirit that will dominate the behavior in more than one or two family members. Why do some families have a disproportionate incidence of incest, alcoholism, drug addiction, mental illness, babies out of wedlock, etc.? Sometimes this can be manifested (all too often) even in strong church families. On one occasion I was teaching about **ruling spirits** in families and my father, Rev. Ralph Ellis, stated at the end of the conference that the ruling spirit in his family was alcoholism; his uncles, his brother, and his sons were affected. Notice that his brother and sons were raised in strong Christian homes and were never exposed to any alcoholic beverages growing up. In this family it was not a case of learning by imitation. Apparently, some ancestor in the past made drinking alcoholic beverages his/her god. Ruling spirits are demons given access to families by some ancestor who allowed a certain demon to dominate in a family. (All Spirit-filled believers must continue to war against these generational curses by binding, rebuking, and casting out whatever spirits dominate in his/her family.)

Powers

No one who has a radio, television, CB radio, or walkie-talkie would deny that our atmosphere is full of physical forces that we cannot see but we use every day. These forces are radio waves, infrared waves, ultraviolet waves, gamma rays, and cosmic rays. Further, the atmosphere is full of gases that we do not see, but need, like oxygen and hydrogen and other gases that we would rather not have in great concentrations such as carbon dioxide. We have wind, heat, and cold, which we never see but always can feel. These facts can give you the picture of Satan's **powers.**

Satan has awesome power in general, but he has a special category in his hierarchy called "**powers.**" **Powers** are those forces that Satan and/or his occult workers can control and call forth with sudden effectiveness. It is interesting that **powers** is always plural and always follows "principalities." **Powers** should therefore be viewed in at least two ways. First, picture "hosts" (too numerous to attach a number to) of identical demons on a specific mission. (Picture the migration of birds. Remember, when some birds migrate, the skies are blackened because they are so numerous.) Haven't you at one time or another been in places or regions of the country where you can sense the atmosphere charged with evil discomfort and where the behavior of extreme decadence dominates most of the population? These **powers** may be directed, controlled, and sent forth by one of Satan's powerful **rulers** (princes) assigned to that region.

Or Satan will gradually set the stage for an event, **then saturate the atmosphere with evil powers (like a torrential rain soaking clothing)** to bring about evil and destruction. An example is the Los Angeles riot of 1992 precipitated by the verdict of innocent given to the policemen charged with the beating of Rodney King. Satan had set the stage with covert and overt racism, which included prior police brutality. At the time of the announced verdict of innocence,

Satan seemed to have saturated the area with unrequited, unstoppable violence and rage, which did not or would not discriminate between the innocent and the guilty. This was the work of **powers**—Satan's specialized "hosts" on a mission. No one wins when Satan works. Whenever and wherever you hear of sudden gang violence or rioting including so many people, remember, these are unseen **powers** or evil forces impelling and compelling this behavior.

Secondly, picture other demons (powers) with the special ability to harness energy in the atmosphere, producing sudden climatic changes in the weather. If man can harness and use unseen physical and electrical forces like radio waves (bands), it is obvious that Satan can do it better. Remember, Satan pollutes, perverts, and corrupts the things of God for his own uses. God created the seasons and the weather, including storms, and Satan can initiate some changes in the weather. Picture demons shifting cold air masses with hot air masses to produce a thunderstorm.

In the story of Job, Satan was allowed to attack Job's substance and family. In Job 1:16, Satan caused **fire to fall** and burn up Job's sheep and servants; in verse 19 Satan sent a great wind that destroyed his house, killing his children in the house.

EXAMPLE:

From personal experience, I know that Satan can temporarily control forces in nature. Our youngest daughter was preparing to move into her dormitory room at medical school. On the last occasion when all her belongings were moved into the room, we had every intention of praying in her room as we usually did when we left our children at school, but we did not.

Even though the sun was shining when we arrived at the dormitory (and the weather reports had not indicated any inclement weather), a sudden darkening of the skies occurred, and it began to rain heavily. We had purchased a feather mattress that we planned to return to the store if it was not suitable, and we did not want it to get wet. As soon as the sky darkened and rain began to fall, we rushed from the dorm to the car with the feather mattress. To our surprise, everything cleared up immediately, and the sun came out again as soon as we arrived at the car.

Two days later our daughter moved in.

By the second weekend, our daughter, who has always been confident about her abilities and future, was nervous, restless, and scared. On that Sunday before returning to school, she stated emphatically that she was not going back because, as she stated, she could not stand it. We couldn't figure out the cause of this sudden change, since from early childhood, she had always said that she was going to be a doctor. We prayed, but we recognized that something serious was going on. I took her back to the dormitory.

On Monday night at 9:30, our daughter called and hysterically told me she could not stay in medical school. I said, "Esther, something has happened and you must tell me." Suddenly she recalled (and Satan had sent a mind-blocking spirit to prevent her from telling me before) that on the prior Thursday, "something was in my room; then it was in the bed with me, and I started pleading the **Blood of Jesus** and it passed through me."

I called one of the prayer warriors, and we IMMEDIATELY went to the dormitory to my daughter's room. As we began to pray, we felt a terrible presence and heaviness in the room which did not want to leave. After praying in the power of the Holy Ghost, those demons taking up residence in that room and attempting to destroy my daughter **were bound, rebuked, renounced, dispossessed, and cast out IN THE NAME OF JESUS OF NAZARETH!!!**

God opened the door and provided the means for my daughter to become a medical doctor. Satan always opposes the plans and the Will of God. He cannot (unless we carelessly allow him) ruin the efficacy of our prayers, but he will do all he can to stop us from praying. God revealed to me afterward that Satan sent the clouds and the sudden rainstorm only long enough for my husband and me to rush from the building (thinking we were avoiding getting drenched and having the mattress ruined), and we forgot to pray. Satan also knew, as in the past, that the Holy Spirit would have made us sensitive to the evil in that dormitory room. Satan knew that his demons in that room would have been exposed if we had begun to pray. He orchestrated the weather situation (powers) to keep us from praying. (Also, to this very day, I am convinced that Satan orchestrated all of the above and had my daughter assigned to a room that a Satanist had lived in.) The Word of God reminds us:

> *"No weapon that is formed against thee shall prosper.[17] ...This is the heritage of the servants of the Lord..."* (Isa. 54:17)

Powers in Creatures of Evil and /or Filth

God gives all types of gifts and abilities. No one would deny there are some individuals with the uncanny ability to train circus animals or run obedience schools for domestic animals. Further, there are others who can charm poisonous snakes without danger to themselves. Satan, who imitates God, is in charge of everyone who has not submitted to God and accepted Jesus as Lord. He is able to use individuals with specialized **witchcraft power to call forth** a profusion of rats, mosquitoes, flies, and snakes to hinder, frighten, intimidate, discourage, or torment individuals, particularly Christians. It is possible that each rat, mosquito, or fly can be inhabited by a separate demon. Recall that the demons that were cast out of the demoniac at Gadara desired to go into the swine (Mark 5:1-14).

---

17   This word "prosper" as it is used in this scripture suggests "succeed."

EXAMPLE

Evangelist John David Lawrence, with one of the praying mothers, went to Atlanta to begin a mission. He had a dream about snakes after he arrived in the area. Unknown to him, he was in an area dominated by individuals practicing the occult. On the evening they were planning to begin outdoor services, while walking toward the designated area, they saw a huge snake slithering rather rapidly toward them. As Evangelist Lawrence could humorously relate some experiences, he stated he was petrified with fear and wanted to run until he realized (IN A HURRY) who he was and who he BELONGED TO: **JESUS**. He and his prayer partner immediately began to pray. **"SATAN, I TAKE AUTHORITY OVER YOU IN THE NAME OF JESUS, I BIND AND REBUKE EVERY DEMON AND SPELL AND SNAKE YOU SEND AGAINST US, AND WE SEND THEM BACK WHERE THEY CAME FROM IN JESUS' NAME!!!"** The huge snake turned and left. GOD SANCTIONED THAT FIRST MEETING WITH A GREAT REVIVAL.

EXAMPLE

I was at a prayer breakfast where Pastor C.R. Johnson of Brooklyn (now deceased) was speaking of a mission trip to India. He stated that just as he was beginning to speak in an outdoor service to thousands of Hindus, the air became thick with flies (getting in their eyes, mouth, and nose). He asked the minister who had invited him, "What is this?" The minister replied, **"Witchcraft."** Pastor Johnson immediately rebuked the **powers of witchcraft;** the swarms of flies left immediately.

Some persons with greater satanic power than others in Satan's service will use this damnable ability against other less powerful servants of Satan as indicated in the following example.

EXAMPLE

A female pastor in Brooklyn had received a considerable number of boxes of designer clothing, which she was selling at very reasonable prices. We had visited her several times. On one occasion, with some of my coworkers, my sister and I went to her church to look at this clothing. When we arrived, we found the place infested with huge ugly rats (**which was not the case on prior visits).** Everyone except my sister and I were frightened, including the pastor and her nieces. Everyone stood trembling on chairs.

This pastor was a spiritualist and apparently some "rival" was "sending" an attack—an army of fat rats. We overheard her consulting with her nieces about sending for reinforcements, an aunt with more "powerful stuff." While they were talking, still standing on chairs, my sister and I got brooms and started **PLEADING THE BLOOD OF JESUS.** The rats left and stayed gone while we were there. We shopped, prayed over the clothing, and sent them to the cleaners before wearing them. The scary spiritualist later told my sister, "Your sister has a lot of power."

The Bible clearly, explicitly, and succinctly states that Jesus has given us power to "tread on serpents and scorpions," or in other words anything that is sent to endanger the believer's life (Luke 10:19).

Rulers of Darkness of This World

There are **"five-star generals"** or special **"rulers"** who are responsible for specific areas of evil. The most obvious areas where these special **rulers** dominate are places like prisons and some psychiatric hospitals. In the literal sense, **"rulers of darkness"** will include all those demons with special responsibility in individuals for relentless violence like Pol Pot, head of the Khmer Rouge of Cambodia (responsible for as many as 3,000,000 deaths), and Idi Amin of Uganda (responsible for 500,000 deaths). Further, there are **rulers** who are specifically assigned to foster drugs, prostitution, pornography, gambling, etc.

All of these **generals or rulers** have hosts of lesser demons with special tasks. For example, the **ruler** of the destructive illegal and legal drugs will send out a cadre of demon spirits with chemical knowledge who will enter or inject satanic wisdom into "open" individuals on how to process cocaine or heroin faster and better or how to create new drug formulae, for example, the at-home production of methamphetamine.

Satan's kingdom is so well organized that the **"ruling princes"** over nations can call for the support from any of the **rulers of darkness** that they need for a specific purpose or a specific location. It is not by chance that drug use and the incidence and prevalence of murder in the East New York community of Brooklyn exceeds all other communities in New York City; the seeds of poverty, alienation, hopelessness, and despair made the desire for drugs or "escape" paramount in the lives of many of this community's residents. The prince over America, GREED, provides the necessary demonic support system.

Spiritual Wickedness in High Places

Some Bible translations called the high places "the heavenlies." To clarify the words **heavenlies or high places**, there needs to be a location description. It is safe to say that the **heavenlies or high places** are those regions up in the atmospheric heavens where **spiritual wickedness** is free to operate (especially when there are no fervent, effectual prayers of the saints).[18] Although Satan is not in the heaven of heavens where God's throne is, it should be understood he does operate in the atmospheric heavens and that there are not only powerful demonic **rulers (princes)** ruling nations or regions, but also highly specialized demons with uniquely special "spiritual" responsibility. The key to understanding **spiritual wickedness in the heavenlies** is that all levels and orders of demons are interacting and planning the destruction

---

18   The earth's atmosphere includes the ionosphere, troposphere, stratosphere, mesosphere, and thermosphere, which constitute over 1,500 vertical miles of gaseous layers and gravity.

of each individual, family, community, and nation. Yes. There is a hierarchy under each **ruler** over each nation— spirits that dominate regions, communities, and families. Some demons are subject to more powerful demons. Note that these demonic forces may have levels of authority, but all are in absolute agreement to destroy as many communities, churches, families, and individuals as possible.

A spiritual void was left in man when he "fell" in the Garden of Eden. Satan, knowledgeable that only God Himself can fill this spiritual void, uses all kinds of spiritual error and evil, including special rituals, doctrinal beliefs, drugs, and emotional experiences of every type to block man from God. These strategies are planned, orchestrated in an on-going convention of spiritual wickedness in high places— sending forth demons of false gods, false belief, deceiving rituals, emotionally delusional experiences, and maintaining an umbrella of deception and clouds of darkness over entire nations.

For example, consider the seven churches of Asia (Smyrna, Ephesus, Pergamos, Thyatira, Sardis, Philadelphia, and Laodicea) located in today's Turkey. These churches were evangelized by the Apostle Paul, and John, the apostle, pastored the mother church at Ephesus for over two years. Christ warned these churches against losing their fervor, against false teachers, against compromising with immorality, against idolatry, against spiritual weakness, etc. (Rev. 2, 3). Read carefully the New Testament writings in the book of Jude. These first-century churches degenerated into apostasy with erroneous preaching, allowing powerful lust demons to operate in the congregations, going after money, etc.

The Spirit of God and the Word of God are THE ULTIMATE AUTHORITY for THE CHURCH OF GOD. When the church refuses or fails to *"hear what the Spirit is saying to the church,"* **the church fails.**

The first-Century church eventually failed. It is no wonder that Turkey and Arabia, which had powerful Christian communities, **are now solidly Moslem.** The disobedience and slothfulness of those early Christian communities in Asia gave Satan legal rights to those regions. He was able to take a willing vessel in the seventh century A.D., Mohammed,[19] invest him with revelations from Allah,[20] (one of Satan's religious dominions ruling in the heavenlies), and organize a powerful world religion BECAUSE THE SAINTS FAILED TO MAINTAIN THE GLORIOUS **LIGHT OF THE GOSPEL.** Think about how difficult it is to evangelize any predominantly Moslem country. Although Christian missionaries continue evangelizing Moslem countries, conversions are rare, as well as dangerous for any Christian convert. These countries are saturated with a religious fervor that absolutely denies the deity and the redemptive message of Christ.

Many traditional practices are pervasive and evil: A female will be killed if she has been raped or committed fornication; young boys are conditioned to become suicide bombers; and death will be certain if you speak negatively of their founder, Mohammed. The "prayer cover" of a few Christian

---

19   Mecca in Saudi Arabia was a predominantly Christian community at the time of Mohammed's birth.

20   One of which was the Jihad or Holy War, with the slogan everyone must bow to Islam or suffer slavery and/or death.

missionaries in some of these Moslem, Hindu, and Buddhist countries is so rare and weak that it rarely affects the saturation of "demons of religious delusion" because of the well-organized **spiritual wickedness in the heavenlies**—levels and layers of demonic forces.

However, the scripture informs us that we have a *"...great high priest that is passed into the heavens..."* (Hebrews 4:14) because *"He that descended is the same also that ascended up far above all heavens..."* (Eph. 4:10). Notice that Jesus was *"...made higher than the heavens"* (Hebrews 7:26), but in the heavens I Peter 3:22 the scripture precisely states that Christ *"...is gone into heaven, and is on the right hand of God; angels and authorities and powers BEING MADE SUBJECT UNTO HIM.*" He is waiting and welcoming all powerful and prayerful believers to pierce the darkness in the heavenlies with their prayers as well as triumphing over evil around them.

We know that God is everywhere all at the same time, but these scriptures suggest that He rules, He mediates, He advocates for saints in the heavens (Hebrews 8:1). This is a reasonable deduction when the Word clearly indicates that Satan comes before God to accuse the brethren (Rev. 12:10) and petition God (in this level of the heavens) for the souls of the saints (Job 1:7:11).[21] When the people of God pray, God dispatches angels to answer (Hebrews 1:14; Dan. 10:10-13) from His throne in the heaven of heavens. On the

---

21 This also makes sense when we realize that the present heavens and earth will pass away. It is obvious that no place where Satan or his authorities, dominions, and rulers have operated will be permitted to remain. (See II Pet. 3:10, Rev. 20:11.)

other hand, when the people of God fall short of praying, it gives Satan THE LEGAL RIGHT to oppress, devour, and destroy by any and all means possible.

When you look at the flux and flow of history and religious movements of the world, you can see how **spiritual wickedness in high places** produces evil, blocking forces in the heavenlies to prevent the light of the Gospel from shining through. The main purpose of "wickedness in the heavenlies" is to deceive and seduce by all means possible. If you read Ephesians 1:17-21 very carefully and consider over and over again what has been written, you will understand that there are powerful evil princes and rulers operating in the earth and in the heavens, but God has given **ALL BELIEVERS DIVINE AND IMMEDIATE ACCESS** to POWER greater than Satan's massive legions of demons.

> *"...That the God of our LORD JESUS CHRIST, the glorious FATHER, may give you the SPIRIT OF WISDOM and REVELATION so that you may know him better. I pray also that the EYES of your HEART may be enlightened in order that you may know the HOPE to which he has called you, the RICHES OF HIS GLORIOUS INHERITANCE in the saints, and HIS incomparably GREAT POWER for us who believe. That POWER is like the working of HIS MIGHTY STRENGTH, which HE EXERTED in Christ when HE RAISED HIM FROM THE DEAD and seated Him at His right hand in HEAVENLY REALMS FAR ABOVE all rule and authority, power and dominion, and every title."* (Eph. 1:17-21)

Spiritual ignorance and **unbelief** are dangerous demons (Hosea 4:6; Rev. 21:8). Until the saints begin to understand and believe in the great **POWER** that is within them because they have received **GOD'S INCOMPARABLY GREAT POWER (which is like His Mighty Strength), THE RESURRECTION POWER (the Holy Ghost),** Satan will continue to have some victories over God's people. Jesus specifically stated, *"...the Kingdom of God is **WITHIN YOU"** (Luke 17:21). Since the Spirit of God resides within the Christians, signs will follow, not staged, forced, or faked, **but follow the believers' life** because of the awesome power of the Holy Ghost **WITHIN THE BELIEVER** (Mark 16:17, 18).

Notice that in Christian nations, the **spiritual wickedness** operating in the heavenlies has a very different method of opposing the Light of the Gospel. Demons of spiritual conspiracy, delusion, and deception will infiltrate the very core of Christianity. The Masons are an excellent example.

THE MASONS

Many Masonic orders require initiates to be Christian, while many of the oaths and rituals are cultic and satanic, anti- Christian:

1. Every grand lodge has a **"most worshipful master."** IS he MORE "WORSHIPFUL" THAN CHRIST?

2. A Master Mason makes a solemn oath <u>on a Bible</u> that he will *"acknowledge and obey ALL DUE SIGNS*

AND SUMMONS SENT TO ME FROM A Master Masons' Lodge or given me by a brother of that degree, if within the length of my cable-tow." And he finishes with "*All this I most solemnly and sincerely promise and swear... so help me God.*" More of this includes that **if he breaks any part of this oath, he will have his body severed in two and disemboweled.**[22]

3. In the York Rite, which is supposed to be more Christian than secular, the **"higher bodies"** become more secretive (these Masons are exposed to more secret knowledge). In the Royal Arch Degree, for example, the candidate is taken through elaborate rituals in the supposed ruins of Solomon's Temple, and discovers the supposed "lost Ark of the Covenant." The candidate finds the so-called "Grand Omnificent Royal Arch Word" for God. The name is **JAH-BUL-ON** and declared to be the Word as found in John 1:5. Look at Satan's deception on the so-called lost name.

JAH, the first syllable, represents Yahweh or Jehovah, the God of Abraham, Isaac, and Jacob.

BUL, the second syllable, represents Baal, the god of Jezebel and Ahab—Israel's most wicked queen and king (I Kings 16:29-33).

ON, the third syllable, represents the name of the

---

22   *Coil's Masonic Encyclopedia,* Macoy Publishing, Richmond, VA. 1961. (p. 51).

Egyptian sun god, the god of Pharaoh. It is the name of his sacred city in Egypt (Genesis 41:45:50).

"Thou shalt not take the name of the Lord thy God in vain; for the Lord will not hold him guiltless that taketh his name in vain." (Exodus 20:7)

Masonry is part occult, part blasphemous, and non-Christian; for the Lord Himself said, *"...for how should my name be polluted? And I will not give my Glory unto another"* (Is. 48:11, 42:8).

4. In the Scottish Rite, Knights of East and West (17th degree), there is also a "SACRED WORD," ABADDON, which means "destroyer," and it is another name of Satan, "the angel of the bottomless pit."

"And they had a king over them, which is the angel of the bottomless pit, whose name in the Hebrew tongue is ABADDON, but in the Greek tongue hath his name Apollyon." (Rev. 9:11)

Further, Masonic theology talks about the "Great Architect of the Universe" (T.G.A.O.T.U.) in its references to God. However, Albert Mackey, a Masonic authority, states that God is equally present with the pious Hindu in his temple, the Jew in his synagogue, the Mohammedan in his mosque, and the Christian in his church. The teachings of Albert Pike and Henry Wilson Coil, two other renowned authorities on Masonry, have the same "generic" teaching about God.

Another 33rd-degree Mason writes that "the true Mason is not creed-bound and that as a Mason his religion **MUST BE UNIVERSAL**. The names of Christ, Buddha, or Mohammed mean little, for he recognizes only the light and not the bearer. He worships in any shrine, temple, mosque, or cathedral, realizing the oneness in all spiritual truth."[23]

The issue of secret societies such as Masonry and Eastern Star is worth belaboring because many so-called Christians (born again) are members of these organizations. Furthermore, many of our United States' presidents beginning with George Washington (who was also a slave owner) were Masons.

Suffice it to say that all the good that Masons and Shriners do for hospitals, education, etc. is a deceptive tactic of Satan to make Masons feel righteous. The pollution of this SPIRITUAL CONSPIRACY is worse in evangelical, holiness, and Pentecostal organizations because these churches teach a personal relationship with God (through the Holy Spirit, who is **A GUIDE AND A TEACHER**) and that pledging to any secret society is sin. Unfortunately, not a few ministers and members in many denominations belong to secret societies.

"Know ye not, that to whom ye yield yourselves servants to obey, his servants ye are to whom ye obey; whether of sin unto death, or of obedience unto righteousness." **(Romans 6:16)**

Satan has **a myriad of disciplined demons whose job is**

---

23   *Masonry: Beyond the Light*, p. 48.

to keep man's mind manipulated and to prevent man from using his wisdom to totally turn to God. The nineties' "Gospel of Prosperity" was rife with spiritual deception; "God **wants you rich**," **"Name it and claim it," the "Gospel of Success,"** and **"God wants you happy"** are direct outgrowths of positive mental attitude seminars and books that tell you essentially that **"it is mind over matter."** The deception is so effective because it is a commonly accepted fact (and to some extent true) that a positive attitude about one's ability to succeed is necessary in order to succeed.

These notions of "possibility thinking" and "the power of positive thinking" are like **sorcery** because these ideas suggest that by thinking positively, man can create whatever experience he desires. Napoleon Hill, who made all these ideas popular, was visited for years by **"Ascended Masters"** (powerful and wise demons) who revealed all this to him. His book *Think and Grow Rich* is conceptually dangerous because it **"deifies" the ability of the mind** to bring things to pass. Earnest Holmes' "Science of the Mind," the positive thinking of Norman Vincent Peale,[24] and even the "Possibility Thinking" of Robert Schuller **place more confidence in the individual's ability to think positively, speak positively, and visualize positively than in confidence in God.** This is the doctrine of **The Human Potential Movement** and **The New Age Movement.**[25] These tend to ignore God or diminish God's importance.

---

24 Norman Vincent Peale credits Holmes with his development into a "positive thinker."

25 Read *The Seduction of Christianity* by Dave Hunt and T.A. McMahon (Harvest House Publishers; Eugene, OR).

It is critical to realize that man is a spiritual being and that he needs TO BE RECONCILED BACK TO GOD AS A PERSONAL CHOICE. **This spiritual wickedness emanating from the heavenlies works on man's will and in his mind (soul) to keep man in a willful sinful state, believing in himself more than God.**

Spiritual deceptions are subtle but GREAT. Preachers and evangelists **using their own soul power** and **not the power of the Holy Spirit** when manipulating people's emotions are not really cognizant of the fact that they are operating in Satan's arena of **HYPOCRISY, SELF-CENTEREDNESS, REBELLION, and even ARROGANCE.** Just as the hypnotist or the sorcerer expects certain results, these persons similarly operate successfully with their own soul power,[26] anticipating certain results.

Unfortunately, it appears that the Christian church never considers how spiritual wickedness in heavenly places seduces, deceives, and destroys faith. It will always be levels and layers of demonic forces operating against ministries and individual Christians. For not only are there some ministers who have pledged to secret societies like the Masons, but Satan will put in place his "angels of light" (demonic leaders) in the body who appear to have genuine ministries.

Consider how Satan will deceive and seduce with his "ministry gifts"…

"For the time will come when they will not endure

---

26   Read Watchman Nee's *Latent Power of the Soul.*

sound doctrine; but after their own lusts shall they heap to themselves teachers, having ITCHING EARS; and they shall turn away their ears from the truth, and shall be turned into fables. **"** (II Tim 4:3,4)

"And no marvel; for Satan himself is transformed into an angel of light. Therefore, it is no great thing if his ministers also be transformed as the ministers of righteousness; whose end shall be according to their works." (II Cor. 11:14, 15)

Satan imitates God and will present himself in a "believer," be they ministers, evangelists, preachers, or the laity, as being greatly anointed of the Holy Ghost. These **angels of lights** can give you a Word of Knowledge about you or your family—because Satan (as "prince of the power of the air") has **a familiar spirit** following everyone. These persons empowered by Satan do have supernatural revelation, but it is from Satan, who knows **all of your past and present because of a familiar spirit**.

These **angels of light** can effect healing. If Satan, being the "prince of this world," sends sickness, he will certainly heal if it is to his advantage to do so. It is a "lying wonder" because the healed individual has opened his soul and spirit to demonic domination.

"For the mystery of iniquity doth already work: only he who now letteth will let, until he be taken out of the way... Even him, whose coming is after the working of Satan will ALL POWER AND SIGNS AND LYING WONDERS." (II Thess. 2:7, 9)

EXAMPLE

There is one woman masquerading all over the country as a great evangelist, going around prophesying, healing, speaking "a word of knowledge," etc. In every church that she has gone to, thousands of dollars are raised, regardless of the size of the congregation. Satan used her mightily in one particular city where there are only a few holiness churches. Many of the Christians in this community had a somewhat carnal church culture, always looking for **"a word"** from someone. They had **"itching ears"** and only liked positive prophecies and marveled at **"signs and wonders,"** so Satan sent them what they were looking for. In this woman's demonic campaign of **"slaying people in the spirit,"** e.g., knocking them out on the floor, Satan presented himself in one person (a visitor) in the prayer line—a twenty-eight-year-old female. Satan spoke out of that visitor as she was being prayed for by this "evangelist" and said "I am going to kill her." Of course, the evangelist continued praying, and the woman **DIED IN THAT CHURCH THAT NIGHT.**

The autopsy showed no pathology. **SATAN KILLED THIS VISITOR IN CHURCH.**

No damage control was possible because the police confiscated the tape of the service, and the news on television carried the story by stating *"a woman killed in exorcist rite in church."* It is now in the public record in the court. A number of spiritual things resulted from this horror:

a) Respect and confidence in holiness churches in this city became almost null and void.

b) The saints became afraid of anything to do with Satan. Their fear of Satan is obvious; they are afraid to use the authority of the Name of Jesus to **rebuke, bind**, and **cast out** demons.

c) The residue of Satan's filth remaining in the church killed the anointing in the church.

d) Some church members, who Satan's **"angel of light"** (the evangelist) prayed for, came under such mental torment, nervous breakdowns occurred. (Satan knows everything you were exposed to and given an opportunity will use those things against you.) When this **witch** (masquerading as an evangelist) prayed for another woman, all the horrible things that happened in her family and in her childhood came back to her ALL AT ONCE. Her mind could not take it, and she had a mental breakdown and had to be hospitalized. **Satan is not merciful**[27]**; he means to kill, steal, and destroy (John 10:10).**

This same witch (masquerading as an evangelist) has traveled all over this country with **signs** and **lying wonders**, raising substantial amounts of money for the church and herself. Every church that she "ministered" in has been in a low spiritual state since. Inevitably, a certain kind of darkness

---

27   **GOD IS MERCIFUL.** He will only allow those things that were blocked out of your mind to come up when you are able to deal with them.

has descended on those churches, and only **repentance and rededication** by the pastor and congregation will free them from this **seduction of darkness.**

Satan is still winning in some of these churches because it is so hard for holiness folk to repent for being involved intentionally or unintentionally in witchcraft—**denial is demonic.**[28] Paul wrote in II Thess. 2:2, 3:

"That ye be not soon shaken in mind, or be troubled, neither by spirit, nor by word, ...LET NO MAN DECEIVE YOU BY ANY MEANS; for that day shall not come, except there come a falling away first..."

The basic thing that leads people into error is the desire to receive some special revelation from God without having a commitment to consecration—**the "itching ear" syndrome.** Further, people love "signs and wonders" and receiving "a word." The Bible is a more than adequate revelation. If the Word gets in you and you are in the Word, you can make it if **you never get a word from anyone or if you never see any signs and wonders.**[29]

---

28 **Denial** is just a euphemism for lying to oneself. Satan is a liar, the father of all lies (John 8:44); when any individual lies to himself/herself, he/she is cooperating with Satan.

29 Signs and wonders never saved anyone. They just demonstrated the power of God to help bring sinners to repentance. Saints do not need signs and wonders, but those who do have the "sin of unbelief" (Rev. 21:8). Remember, all the miracles that Jesus performed in His earthly walk were seen by His followers and others. But the wonders did not mean anything to them at the time of His crucifixion; He was left alone.

Spiritual wickedness in the heavenlies will infuse the church with *seducing spirits*. "Seduce," or "seduction," derives from the Greek work "seductus," meaning to "a leading apart or astray." "Seduced" means "to be taken by the hand and led slowly in the wrong direction." A person follows because he/she trusts and believes in the person leading. **Seducing spirits** will work on believers RIGHT IN THE CHURCH to **keep the mind and the emotions looking for something greater and more interesting.** If believers are prayerful and watchful, they can be aware of potential evil or seductions from individuals (even preachers, evangelists, or pastors).

Consider how Satan will deceive and seduce with DOCTRINE...

Satan's array of demons operating in religious institutions as well as in individuals have special **seducing spirits** to work with church doctrines. Quite often, the person who a **seducing spirit** is using is <u>deceived also</u>. Being seduced, therefore, is not a sudden change in behavior, belief, or intent, but a gradual process. This "leading astray" can often be observed in movements based on a single focus; for example, **eternal security** from John 10:28, 29 or **snake-handling churches** from Mark 16:18. However, Satan is doing a new but subtle thing. Churches that are perceived as preaching the full gospel have specialized in certain areas that are openings for Satan. Some of these churches worship their doctrines and religious practice more than God.

Some subtle deceptions...

In certain charismatic circles, **studying and knowing the**

Word seem to be emphasized **more than living it.** Bible study becomes the main focus of Christian service. Speaking the Word demonstrates faith; the favorite scripture is Mark 11:23, 24. Commitment in these churches means that members devote themselves to the study of the Word. Greater commitment is starting a Bible study group in the home. Rarely is **sanctification** emphasized. Satan knows the Word and will help anyone to specialize in the Word as long as they are not living it and don't truly believe it (e.g., some seminaries teach that Mary, the Mother of Jesus, was not a virgin and the Book of Jonah is just an allegory).

Numerous churches stress and believe that if you speak "in tongues" (glossolalia), it is from God. Therefore, the zenith of their Christian experience is to exhibit the "gift of tongues." In some churches, seekers are actually told to begin speaking whatever they hear, and that will be the Holy Ghost. <u>Satan loves this and will help the spiritually innocent and/or ignorant to speak in HIS OTHER TONGUES—a tongue unknown to you and everyone in the room, which could be cursing God and the church.</u>

EXAMPLE

My sister, daughter, and I were ministering at a retreat, where as soon as anyone began praying, everyone began babbling in tongues. They were taught to pray in **THEIR OWN PRAYER LANGUAGE (notice the emphasis).** When I began praying at the end of a session on the first day, I had to stop because I felt nauseated because of the unclean spirits in the room. I called back to New York for a coworker in the gospel, Evangelist Nellie Harper, and another one of my daughters to come and assist us. On the last day, it appeared that everyone who was ministered to had some demons. **It was a battle!** Women were howling, screaming, gagging, and vomiting as those demons were bound and cast out IN THE NAME OF JESUS. Hatred, murder, lust, lesbianism, and even witchcraft were exposed and defeated that day. **(BUT EVERYONE WAS PRAYING IN THEIR OWN PRAYER LANGUAGE—IN TONGUES!)**

In churches that make the speaking in tongues the peak of their religious experience, people are seduced into believing they are filled with the Holy Ghost when they haven't even sanctified themselves. This **tongue-speaking religious demon** feeds on pride because **tongue-speaking** is visible and audible.

1. First of all the Holy Ghost only comes into a **clean life** (II Cor. 10:11). Speaking in unknown tongues should edify, strengthen, and build the believer up (I Cor. 14:4).

2. If you have not sanctified yourself (including your thought life) while trying to learn how to speak in tongues, you have just sent a carte blanche invitation to Satan's religious demons.

3. He, the Holy Ghost, gives the utterance, not you. **If you can pray in tongues or speak in tongues anytime you get ready to, it is either your own made-up tongue or Satan's tongues.** The Holy Ghost is

not like a light switch, to be turned on and off to suit your convenience.

4. An unknown tongue that causes a break in the service must be interpreted. Of course, some make up tongues and make up interpretations (I Cor. 14:27, 28).

THESE PEOPLE ARE IN DANGER BECAUSE:

a) They are opening their souls continuously to the **powers of darkness.**

b) It will become harder and harder for them to repent and receive the Holy Spirit in His fullness.

The churches that emphasize tongues make it harder and harder for the Holy Spirit to minister in these churches. Consequently, you will note that these churches must invite in prophets, healers, many gifted and dynamic speakers to keep the people entertained.

Another great error is seen in ministries that seem to be built on **laying on of hands** and **slaying people in the Spirit. Laying on of hands** is Biblical and instituted by God.[30] The **laying on of hands** is a method of ministering the Spirit or transferring the anointing. But it seems empty of spiritual relevance if everyone falls on the floor and there is no change in the individuals; the "slayee" ought to be healed, changed, delivered, or at least see a vision of God.

---

30   See James 5:14,15; Acts 14:3; Acts 28:8.

Sometimes even in a normal church service, you can have some demons transferred by the laying on of hands.

EXAMPLE

One sister laid her hands on a woman's back while praying for her in service. Almost immediately the sister who was prayed for experienced a back problem that was very painful. After two weeks of prayer and fasting, that "spirit of infirmity" left her back.

There are other churches that seem to emphasize praising God as the doctrinal center of their faith. Praise is comely for the people of God, and God does deserve all the glory and praise, but sometimes these "praise ministries" inadvertently suggest that God can be bribed with praise to receive whatever is desired. This is a diversionary gospel in that there may be times you never receive particular answers to petitions (I Peter 4:12-14). Because God truly loves every believer, He cannot and will not give everything each believer wants or thinks he/she needs. If believers did receive everything petitioned for, it could destroy them spiritually.

Nevertheless, Satan can and does work through a praise ministry. What he does is **lift (temporarily) the depression, the loneliness, the anger, the hate, etc. so that the person can feel better momentarily.** Then he works hard to keep the church **busy with new programs, prophecies, and praise services so that the person will never learn how to identify their spiritual deficits nor how to "pray through" for his/ her own needs, be it for help and deliverance for himself, his family, church, or others.** So weekly or biweekly, the believers will return for doses of "praise **therapy**" or "praise **relief**" instead of **Holy Ghost empowerment to dispossess Satan from their territory.** Remember, DELIGHTING YOURSELF IN GOD according to Psalm 37:4 IS NOT LIMITED TO PRAISE RITUALS. **Delighting yourself in God is a lifestyle.**

Unfortunately, these believers are seduced into **spiritual complacency** because the praise services are absolutely exhilarating and emotionally satisfying, but complacency can be the precursor for spiritual death. Spirits (demons) seduce the people of God to remain in the comfort zone while the **UNSEEN WAR CONTINUES RELENTLESSLY.** Observe how these **"comfort demons"** operate…

Spiritual Complacency

- Not realizing that consecration and revival are not necessarily dependent on the pastor's decisions.

- Not realizing that when Jesus said *"Occupy until I come"* (Lu. 19:13-26), He meant for every Christian to consistently pray, study the Bible, and witness. (When the saint does not OCCUPY, Satan **"occupies"** the territory; the home, the church, and the community.)

Spiritual Ignorance

- Not realizing that Satan works **ALL THE TIME** (even in dreams)**,** especially in the atmosphere of spiritual weakness, greed, competition, fear, etc.

- Not understanding that the judgment or wrath of God is going to be worse for the people of God who failed than for the sinner who never knew God.

Spiritual Blindness

- Not discerning how Satan is manipulating the church and individuals through power struggles.

- Not discerning how Satan can bring individuals into bondage because of submission to the wrong persons for the wrong reasons.

- Not discerning that God longs to, desires to, and is willing to have every child of God saturated in His anointing for "kingdom work" (Eph. 1:15-23).

The deceptions wrought through the hierarchy of **spiritual wickedness in the heavenlies,** to keep man from the spiritual reality and fullness of God, are seemingly endless. There is a whole range of polluted Christian belief like that which is taught in spiritualist churches. The dabbling in astrology, false prophets (I John 4:1), and false Christs showing "signs and wonders" (Matt. 24:24), false apostles, false ministers (II Cor. 11-13-15); all are directed from the **spiritual wickedness** in the heavenlies. Satan backs up these evil spiritual laborers with **lying wonders:** For example David Koresh calling himself Christ in Waco, Texas, precipitating the death of scores of people; from Los Angeles, California, Jim Jones took more than 900 people to Guyana and compelled them to commit suicide.

"For false Christs and false prophets shall rise and shall shew signs and wonders, TO SEDUCE if it were possible, even the elect." (Mark 13:22)

SATAN'S VISIBLE OPERATION

An examination of Satan's operation will demonstrate his devious, perniciously foul, consistent devices that he uses to destroy individuals, churches, communities, and nations. Even though Satan has a well-organized hierarchy directed by him, working diligently for him, and reporting back to him (as discussed above), there needs to be a discussion of how Satan operates through individuals with the gifts God gave him when he was created by God as Lucifer. Because he was on the Holy Mount of God with splendor and beauty, he still has phenomenal ability that may be beyond man's comprehension. His gifts were not taken from him; he corrupted them.

- His **beauty** (Ezekiel 28:12)

- His **wisdom** (v.12)

- His **garments** or outer layers of precious stones and metals (v.13)

- His **music**; tabrets and pipes (v.13)

- His **perfection** (v.15)

- His **brightness** (v.17)

Once Satan's original beauty, brilliance, and brightness are understood, the scripture explaining some of his maliciousness is understood likewise.

"And no marvel, for Satan himself is transformed into an angel of light. Therefore it is no great thing if his ministers will also be transformed as the ministers of righteousness..." (II Cor. 11:14, 15)

How does Satan use BEAUTY to *steal, kill, and destroy?*

Notice first of all how the scripture addresses the work of Satan...

"For all that is in the world, THE LUST OF THE FLESH, AND THE LUST OF THE EYES and THE PRIDE OF LIFE, is not of the Father, but is of the world." (I John 2:16)

"...For all these worldly things, these evil desires— the craze for sex, the ambition to buy everything that appeals to you, and the pride that comes from wealth and importance—these are not from God. They are from this evil world itself." (I Jo. 2:16, **Living Bible)**

How Satan Operates with Beauty

Many people are dissatisfied with their personal appearance, finding themselves either too fat, too skinny, too short, too tall, or just having too many lumps in the wrong place. The ideal is represented by a youth cult of slimness, shapeliness, and the Eurocentric ideal of beauty. Therefore in the media beautiful, sensuous women and handsome men sell cars, soft drinks, alcohol, toilet paper, household cleaning products, toothpaste, jeans, etc. Unfortunately, most things seem to be advertised with blatantly serious sexual overtones. Beauty sells sex. Sex sells everything. Therefore all the marketing constantly associated with sex and beauty is helping weaken the moral fabric of this nation.

On aerobic exercise shows, muscular, handsome males and thin, shapely females are flipping, flopping, and hopping with enviable ease. Satan's object then is to reinforce the **"spirit of rejection"** in most people. Those gorgeous, perfect-looking people in the media and advertising are the abnormal; the normal are the people who are of all shapes, colors, heights, weights, hair and skin types, who also keep their lumps in the wrong places. The subliminal suggestion of the beautiful youth cult is to lie to you in numerous ways.

1) To make you feel that you are a physical misfit.

2) To make you believe that somehow the consumption of those advertised items will make you feel better, look better, act better, etc.

3) To make you feel like your mate of ten or fifteen years may not be the right one, after all.

Strange, isn't it, that the professional call girls, who are exceptionally elegant and beautiful, are often models who did not make it in the professional modeling world. They could not sell their beauty one way, but they were able to sell it another way. Notice that anyone who is exceptionally beautiful and shapely is more often than not advised to make money off their looks. However, the agenda of Satan is to corrupt every good thing, even physically gorgeous people.

"For he seethe that wise men die, likewise the fool, and the brutish person perish, and leave their wealth to others... Like sheep they are laid in the grave; death shall feed on them...and their beauty shall consume in the grave from their dwelling." (Psalm 49:10-14)

Consider the Marilyn Monroes (the beautiful people) in the entertainment world who market their beauty but cannot handle the disappointment and the fallout that their beauty courted.

"Charm is deceptive, and beauty is fleeting..." (Prov. 31:30)

How Does Satan Use His Wisdom?

Wisdom is defined as "an understanding of what is true, right, or lasting," and "common sense" or "good judgment." The origin and basis for all wisdom is God. Therefore we read in Proverbs, *"The fear of the Lord is the beginning of wisdom"* (9:10). Further, *"...the fear of the Lord, that is wisdom; and to depart from evil is understanding* (Job 28:28). On the other hand, Satan profanes his wisdom, which originated in God: *"...thou has **CORRUPTED** thy wisdom by reason of* *thy brightness"* (Ezekiel 28:17).[31]

"To corrupt" means

1. To destroy or subvert honesty and integrity

2. To ruin morally; to pervert

3. To taint; contaminate; infect

4. To cause to become rotten; to spoil

Satan works with well-thought-out plans, using subterfuge and deceit. He will never tell you—nor will administrators and teachers in the public schools, the universities and colleges, or the church community—that *"I am working continuously to infiltrate the institutions and organizations with my corrupted wisdom."*

1. The Media

By the time a child is school age, he is already open to occultism and mysticism; the innocent child's world view has already been molded into accepting New Age dogma. The cartoons on Saturday morning not only glorify "good" witches, wizards, and sorcerers, but the schools are now giving children assignments to research their astrological signs. Children eventually accept many shows and celebrations as normal, even dressing like witches on Halloween.

---

31 *"...And you corrupted your wisdom because of your splendor"* (Ezekiel 28:17, NIV).

2. The Schools

Humanist educators have been gradually eliminating and deliberately censoring basic facts of American History as it relates to America's Christian foundation. While the teachers will teach about the Sun god or Earth Mother goddess of other religions, Christianity cannot be taught. However, "values clarification," a humanist and New Age ideology (find the real you and do what you want for the real you) is commonplace instruction in the classrooms.

In addition, children are taught relaxation techniques, meditation, and channeling (letting a special friend help you—**a demon**). Some elementary schools are using Ouija boards, and showing children how to read palms.[32] Sadly, teachers who are not into the New Age Movement, nor witches, nor Satanists, are encouraged to teach students relaxation techniques and visualization to improve behavior and learning. (Relaxation techniques, meditation, and visualization teach individuals how to discipline themselves to have a "passive mind.") Just like the drug addict who poisons his brain with crack cocaine and other chemicals, and loses control of his thinking faculties, encouraging children concerning meditating and relaxing their minds really gives Satan access to their minds, allowing demons to walk in and take up residence there.[33]

---

32   Every parent, grandparent, surrogate parent, and foster parent needs to read *Lambs to the Slaughter*, by Johanna Michelson (Harvest House, Eugene, OR. 1989).

33   *Sorcery* is translated from the word *pharmakia*, which also translates to drugs or medicine.

In a conversation with a nephew, who is a teacher and testifies to being saved from his sins, he related to me that he teaches relaxation techniques, saying nothing is wrong with this because the students improved in behavior and performance in the classroom. Satan is a **lying wonder** and will wondrously improve behavior and learning while opening the children to demonic control without them or their parents realizing this.

Our institutions of learning are **CORRUPTED WITH SATAN'S WILES AND WISDOM.** In HIGHER EDUCATION (colleges and universities), witchcraft and the occult are called parapsychology, a subdivision of the department of psychology in some universities, and of anthropology in others. Highly respected disciplines such as neurophysiology and theoretical physics have committed themselves to research the manifestations of mediums, yoga, psychic surgeons, sorcerers, witches, and shamans—all in the name of scientific investigation. However, these institutions' administrators and professors fervently deny involvement in the occult.

The key point is that witchcraft is a "legitimate" discipline in universities and colleges, and it is taught and demonstrated. One can sit in on séances, observe levitation, and verify extrasensory perception in the classroom.

A growing phenomenon in colleges and universities all over the United States is the growing and popular Harry Potter competitions, imitating some of the behavior in the Harry Potter books and films. One of the competitions includes races with brooms (presumably like witches) between their legs.

"Let no man deceive himself. If any man among you thinketh himself to be wise in this world, let him become a fool, that he may be wise. For the wisdom of this world is foolishness with God. For it is written, He taketh the wise in their own craftiness. And again, the Lord knoweth the thought of the wise that they are vain." (I Cor. 3:18-20)

In these times, young people need to comprehend all levels of reality prior to going away to any secular institution. Before they go to these universities, they need to know that some of the things being taught are absolutely opposed to Christian teaching and dogma. If the student has not been adequately prepared for some of this New Age and parapsychology teaching, he/she may be walking in Satan's territory to be spiritually overwhelmed by evil, **WITHOUT REALIZING IT.**

EXAMPLE

I was invited to minister to students and professors (by The Christian Fellowship) at a very prestigious women's college in the New England area, which began as an evangelical school for women. As we (Nellie Harper, my sister, Joy Walker, and I) arrived on this beautiful campus, with gorgeous gothic buildings and beautifully landscaped gardens, we were immediately nauseated. Our IMMEDIATE response was *"What is going on here?"*

The students looked depressed, oppressed, and worn out. Some were obviously doing drugs and into alternative lifestyles. As I attempted to pray and teach, it was as though I was in a vacuum by myself. I was not immediately aware of the problem. Realizing something was not right, I mentioned to my coworkers, "Let's stop the workshop and do some fervent praying." We began to pray, and the more we prayed, the more difficult it was to pray, and we became extremely physically weak. But we continued to rebuke, bind, and cast out the powers of darkness. As we were praying, **THE LORD REVEALED** that THERE WERE COVENS (like congregations) of WITCHES, including students and professors, strengthening each other in darkened rooms with candles and crystal balls, **RIGHT ON THE CAMPUS.** The Lord also revealed that there was massive ideological witchcraft taking place, that is, "Give the professor in writing what the professor wants or else fail." After warring in the Spirit for a while, the Lord had me ask Sister Harper to open the door. She stated she heard demons leaving that building, screaming and squealing. WE RETURNED TO NEW YORK IMMEDIATELY AFTER THAT SESSION.

Later during the semester, a revival broke out among the Christian fellowship; the young women were delivered from drugs and all forms of sexual promiscuity.[34] One ripple effect included greatly improved grades.

---

34   At this particular school, 40 percent of each graduating class became practicing lesbians while attending this school (personal communication with one of the professors).

3. The Church

The Church absolutely needs persons with administrative skills, music ability, and of course, preaching ability. All too often, however, we find ungodly church workers operating in the church. These persons may have never been saved. They may have come from the outside or may have even been raised in the church. In fact, some may have some highly contemptible worldly lifestyles, but Satan wants them integrated into the higher levels of the church. Satan therefore amplifies, increases, and improves the skills of these ungodly church workers, to such a degree that they appear indispensable.

EXAMPLE

One church had an all-around gifted person who had been raised around the church. He was a gifted administrative type with excellent office skills. He was also the announcer for their weekly broadcast. There was not a day in the week when he was not working in some capacity at the church. This man (an admitted homosexual) was at times vicious and filled with anger and, when he felt like it, would literally curse any of the saints out. On one occasion, he actually took his pants down and told one of the members to kiss his buttocks (only in stronger language). This man had carried on so long, he had to have been reprobate, but he was presumably indispensable.

The above may be extreme in terms of the behavior exhibited, but all over the church world, ungodly, unrighteous people are allowed to serve in almost any capacity in the church. **Just as the praises of the saints allow the habitation of God's Spirit (Psalm 22:3), these persons' activities, speech, and conduct allow Satan's habitation.** God is not going to sanction the unrighteous, but some substitute emotionalism, efficiency, and professionalism, then claim "God is working." Satan's corrupted wisdom has found a place among the righteous and has hindered the freedom of the Holy Spirit in the church.[35]

How Does Satan Use Clothing?

Satan's covering was awesomely beautiful. Since everyone tends toward pride and self-centeredness (the sin nature), this tendency will often show in the way people dress. Evangelicals, Pentecostals, and Holiness folk don't hang out in discos, do not drink, steal, fornicate, lie, etc. But dressing and emphasis toward overdressing seem to be a source of personal gratification (Isaiah 3:16-23; I Tim. 2:9). In the church, Satan not only uses the dressing syndrome and culture to reinforce man's innate pride and self-centeredness, but he uses clothing in other ways.

- He uses clothing to seduce, usually with just enough flesh showing to suggest sexual impropriety. He persuades people to dress as though there is a fabric famine; with clothing too short and too tight.

- He definitely uses clothing to reinforce either

---

35 Read the story of Israel's defeat because of sin in the camp in Joshua 7:1-25.

ignorance, rebellion against norms, or retardation. For example, so many young males wear their pants too large and falling off without belts and laces on their sneakers untied (known as the prison look).

- On the other hand, he will use clothing to deceive. Some Satanists dress to look like sincere saints; no lipstick, long dresses with dark somber colors, head coverings, little or no jewelry and of course, with the Bible in their hand. Satan sends these persons with **'religious demons'** to work as church workers to help ruin the spiritual progress of churches[36].

- He places a lust for clothing and jewelry addiction in people, to destroy their finances and their peace.

How Does Satan Use Music?

One could write volumes on this subject. We know of the persuasive healing power of music, and it is well documented as in the case of David playing to ease Saul's tormented mind (I Sam. 16:14-17, 23). It is obvious that music makes ministry more effective, whether it is an open-air service, Sunday morning worship, or the altar call. It is not difficult to understand how music, which can be so mentally, emotionally, and physically satisfying, can become an important tool of Satan. The statement of Pythagoras, the Greek philosopher, about harmony and man's spiritual existence seems relevant. He taught that melody dealt with man's psychic being (his mind and emotions), rhythm with man's physical life and

---

36   Matthew 7:15.

the functions of the body, and harmony with man's spiritual existence.

Most persons have heard how satanic and devilish the popular extremes in music like heavy metal are. Some musical genres actually charge the atmosphere with aberrant behavior and violence. Since music was created in Satan, he will also use the music in the church to pollute the atmosphere and prevent the Spirit of God from working.

EXAMPLE

I was in a revival where the church had received a real breakthrough; the saints were rejoicing and singing "Victory Is Mine." The Spirit of God was truly in our midst. One of the young people (who should have been trying to get her own breakthrough) switched songs to one of these contemporary gospel songs, with its harsh, discordant harmony in minor chords. The Spirit of God exited, and **"flesh"** was singing and rejoicing.

When these discordant sounds are rendered in church services, either spiritual heaviness ensues or an entertainment atmosphere permeates, which obviously are not of God. Notice that worldliness includes adapting the music of the world to gospel lyrics. Rest assured that God is not going to anoint Satan's music in any worship service. Music should minister the Spirit of God to the hearers and/or set the atmosphere for worshipping the Lord.

"...But be filled with the Spirit, speaking to

yourselves in psalms and hymns and <u>spiritual song,</u>
<u>singing, making melody in your hearts to the Lord.</u>"
(Eph. 5:18b, 19)

Some music in some churches seem to be performed mainly
for its manipulative value, that is, to manipulate emotions or
just for the carnal pleasure of the hearers.

EXAMPLE

I went to a Christmas cantata. Many of our preteens
and teenagers from our church went also. There was
so much rock and hip hop in the Christmas songs being performed that our young people, most of whom
were unsaved, were bouncing and rocking, almost
"boogying down." These young people were sweat-
ing bullets. They loved the music. Yet, there was not
one inkling of worship seen or heard.

Some of the music we hear in church is labeled "contemporary music," "gospel rap," or "gospel rock." Satan does not
care if you are in church playing rock, jazz, or hip hop, as
long as he controls the music. Also some of the musicians
in many churches play for clubs and unsaved groups on
Saturday and then for church services on Sunday. Their music sounds like they forgot that they left the club at daybreak.

A further note on music in the church: Bishop Charles
Harrison Mason, the founding father of the Church of God
in Christ, was opposed to choirs from the church's inception.
He taught that people would come to church waiting to be

entertained instead of singing as unto the Lord.[37]

Even though God has made all believers in the spiritual realm "kings and priests" for Him, believers must never forget Satan is using everything—good, bad, beautiful, indifferent, ugly—in every person, institution, and community to destroy and/or take every person possible to hell with him.

Being a WARRIOR is not an option.

It is a mandate from God!

"The thief [Satan]cometh not, but for to steal, kill and destroy: I am come [Jesus] that they might have life and that they [the believers] might have it more abundantly." **(John 10:10)**

---

37   Personal testimony by Father Ralph N. Ellis, who was a member of the church pastored by Bishop Mason from 1922 to 1936.

MAN, Who Is Man?

God created the heavens, earth, all living things (plants and animals), angels, and Lucifer. At the creation of plants and all living creatures, he placed within each species self-perpetuating instinctual abilities.

"And God said, let the earth bring forth grass, the herb yielding seed, and fruit tree yielding fruit AFTER HIS KIND, whose seed is in itself, upon the earth... And God created great whales, and, every living creature that moveth...AFTER THEIR KIND, and every winged foul AFTER HIS KIND... And God said, Let the earth bring forth the living creature AFTER HIS KIND...Cattle and creeping thing, and beast of the earth AFTER HIS KIND, and it was so." (Gen. 1:11, 21, 22, 24)

But in the 26th verse, God's creation of man was "after God's likeness and in God's image." God **SPOKE** all earth and all living things into existence, but *"...he FORMED man of the dust of the ground."* Moreover, God's care, concern, and love for man were such that He personally *"...BREATHED into his nostrils the breath of life; and man became a living soul"* (Genesis 2:7).

"And God said, Let us make man in our image, af-
ter our likeness: and let them have dominion over
the fish of the sea, over the fowl of the air, and over
the cattle, and over all the earth, and over every
creeping thing that creepeth upon the earth." **(Gen.**
1:26)

And the record states…

"So God CREATED MAN IN HIS <u>OWN</u> IMAGE,
IN THE IMAGE OF GOD CREATED HE HIM;
<u>MALE AND FEMALE</u> CREATED HE THEM."
(Gen. 1:27)

The uniqueness of man's creation is worth stressing to highlight God's great Love for man from the very beginning. Notice that Satan (formerly Lucifer), who had witnessed the creation (Ezekiel 28:13), was already totally evil when God created man. Obviously, Satan witnessed the Love of God during man's creation, where God not only had created a perfect environment for man, but also gave man His Spirit (in order for man to be in a perfect relationship with Him).

God, who is perfectly just and consistent, gave man (just as He did Lucifer and all the angels) a will. Further, he gave man great wisdom to have dominion over everything, because He, God, is wisdom. He also gave man the ability to love and be loved because He, God, is love.[38]

Satan used all of his wisdom and beauty to seduce man into

---

38   See the chapter "Made in the Image of God" in *Called to Be Saints* by
      Fay Ellis Butler, for greater details on the tripartite nature of man.

disobeying God. It should be obvious that Satan, who is doomed for final and total destruction in "outer darkness" and "the lake of fire," will do everything and anything to block and oppose man from receiving God's love and returning God's love. Notice that Satan's success in the Fall of Man in the Garden was only partial and temporary.

"Wherefore, as by one man sin entered into the world, and death by sin; so death passed on all men, for that all have sinned... For if by one man's offence death reigned by one; much more they which receive abundance of grace and of the gift of righteousness shall reign in life by ONE, JESUS CHRIST." **(Romans 5:12, 17)**

WARRING AGAINST SIN

Man's Sin Nature

"For the good that I would do I do not but the evil which I would not, that I do. Now if I do that I would not, it is no more I that do it, but the sin that dwelleth in me. I find a law, that, when I would do good, evil is present with me. For I delight in the law of God after the inward man. But I see another law in my members, warring against the law of my mind, and bringing me into captivity to the law of sin which is in my members." **(Romans 7:19-23)**

Remember, when man was perfectly obedient in a sinless environment, there was no understanding of sin and no desire to sin. Before The Fall in the Garden, the spirit of man was dominant and in a perfect relationship with God.

Man was made in God's image with a will, and with his will man made the choice to disobey God (by eating of the tree of the knowledge of good and evil). Apparently man did not realize that God had given man and woman absolute dominion and control in their perfect environment, and that Satan, the deceiver, had no power over Him (Gen. 1:28). However, Satan was subtle and appeared as a beautiful, seductive, convincing serpent. When man chose to obey Satan and disobey God, he became Satan's seed, and therefore subject to him. In other words, when God was disobeyed and the fruit eaten, Adam abdicated his dominion and power and gave both to Satan. Not only that, Satan became his father. In the same way individuals are genetically similar to their natural fathers without being fully aware of all the intricacies of genetics and inheritance, all individuals receive Satan's seed because of disobedience and sin. The scripture makes this (man's inherited **sin nature** from Satan) clear:

> *"Behold, I was shapen in iniquity; and in sin did my mother conceive me."* **(Psalm 51:5)**

SPIRIT:

> *"Having therefore these promises, dearly beloved, let us cleanse ourselves from all filthiness of the flesh and SPIRIT..."* **(II Cor. 7:1)**

SOUL:

"For they that are after the flesh do mind the things of the flesh; but they that are after the Spirit the things of the Spirit..." (Romans 8:5)

BODY:

"Let not sin therefore reign in your mortal body, that ye should obey it in the lusts thereof." (Romans 6:12)

Previously, man was God-conscious through his spirit; now man became self-conscious through his desires and his pride—his soul.

"For all that is in the world, the lust of the flesh, and the lust of the eyes, the pride of life, is not of the Father, but of the world." (I John 2:16)

God withdrew His Spirit from man's spirit, and a void (spiritual emptiness) was left; because of self-centeredness, man would constantly try to fill the void that only God could satisfy.[39] Man's senses (touching, seeing, hearing, smelling, tasting) would always be gateways to sin. Furthermore, since man broke his covenant with God, he not only was separated from God, but was also placed in an environment that was dominated by Satan (who became the "prince of this world"

---

39   This is the source of addictions of every kind, including sexual addiction, drug and alcohol addiction, gambling addiction, the love of money, etc. Whatever man obtains or secures, the **sin-nature** demands more.

and the "prince of the powers of the air").

Therefore, as soon as you repent, you are in a spiritual war zone. Satan does not want to have the peace of God nor to believe that you can put all of your **flesh** and your **thought life** under the subjection to the Holy Spirit. Satan, who was created full of wisdom, understands completely **the sin nature,** which is to be self-centered, self-serving, self-conscious—**SELFISH and PROUD.** Notice that **self-centeredness** covers the range from **vanity, arrogance, and pride to self-pity, depression, and suicide.** Mentally ill people wallowing in paranoia have become totally self-centered, in other words, the center of their own universe.

"Thus know that in the last days,
perilous times shall come.

Men shall be lovers of their own selves,

covetous,

boasters,

proud,

blasphemers,

disobedient to their parents,

unthankful,

unholy,

without natural affection,

trucebreakers,

false accusers,

incontinent,

fierce,

despisers of those that are good,

traitors,

heady,

high-minded,

lovers of pleasure rather than lovers of God,

HAVING A FORM OF GODLINESS BUT DENYING THE POWER THEREOF." **(II Tim. 3:1-5)**

As long as a born-again Christian lives, he/she will have to deal with the **sin nature**. All too often, persons claiming salvation for five, ten, fifteen, or twenty or more years may never have to deal with the kinds of uncleanness indicated above. Nevertheless, the **sin nature** always tends toward pride, self-centeredness, and selfishness. Look at the many seemingly innocuous ways we allow our **sin nature** to rule.

Question:

1) When you are given too much change after a purchase, do you return it?

2) Do you find yourself among a group of people gossiping, and although you may not be participating, you remain and listen?

3) Do you find yourself preaching, teaching, or doing the most beneficial thing for one's political or social advancement in your organization, even when it is contrary to God's direction?

4) Do you find yourself watching television more than you attend church, studying the Word, or praying?

5) Do you find that when you feel you just may have offended someone, you try being extra nice to them instead of humbling yourself and apologizing? Or, when you do attempt to apologize, you start you statement with *"If I have hurt you..."*?

Your **sin nature** will always keep you doing what you **FEEL LIKE DOING.** When you repented and accepted the Lord, you were freed from not only the penalty and power of sin, but also the dominion of sin.

> *"But he that is joined to the Lord is one spirit... What? Know ye not that your body is the temple of the Holy Ghost which is in you, which ye have of God, and ye are not your own?"* **(I Cor. 6: 17, 19)**

When you heard the Word, accepted the message of redemption, you used your will and mind to make that decision. Because of your willing repentance, God's Spirit was able to take up residence in your spirit.

God, who is absolutely fair and just, still will not violate your will. He allows you, who are no longer under the dominion and power of sin, **freedom to deal with temptations**

and SATAN. Your mind was cleansed by the Blood of Jesus, and your spirit was reconciled back to God (because He has given you His Spirit).

At the time of your conversion and sanctification, you were recreated spiritually. However, you came to the Lord with the composite of THE TOTAL YOU!!! This includes your family relationships (which could have included memories of great tenderness between family members or horrible violence). You also came to the Lord with your personal culture. Suppose you were prone to use profanity before you came to the Lord. Some profanity may slip out after your conversion, but you learn from your experience; you repent and sanctify yourself. Personal sanctification is an ongoing process, but as a Spirit-filled believer, you are equipped to sanctify yourself and continue "growing in Grace."

Also you brought with you all of your personal experience; some you remember, some you do not. Some horrible experiences may have been blocked out of your conscious memory, but they are still imprinted in the subconscious. Recognize that Satan will attempt to weaken you (spiritually) with flashbacks and painful memories of the past[40] if you fail to practice **FORGIVING THOSE WHO HAVE ABUSED, MISUSED, CRITICIZED, BETRAYED, MISTREATED, and OPPOSED you!!!**

Understand the scripture *"neither give place to the devil"* (Eph. 4.27). Satan has a complete record of every experience you have ever had; he knows how to inject evil thoughts into

---

40   See the chapter "The Mind Game," *Called to Be Saints*, by Fay Ellis Butler.

your mind EVEN THOUGH HE CANNOT READ YOUR MIND. Whatever experiences you have had, he recorded the subsequent mood, behavior, and/or words. As soon as these are observed again, he will inject negative thoughts into your mind. *"Neither give place to the devil"* means that you must discipline your mind to think on positive things instead of past torment (Phil. 4:8). Jesus equips the Christian with **"weapons which are not carnal"**—the Name of Jesus, the Word of God, the Blood of Jesus, the Power of Praise, and the Holy Spirit.

Because of living in a sinful world with a nature that is subject to sin, the believer must always sanctify him/herself (I John 5:3). That is why John emphasizes that those who are really committed to God cannot keep sinning.[41]

> *"No one who is born of God will continue to sin, because God's seed remains in him; he cannot go on sinning because he is born of God. This is how we know we are the children of God…"* **(I John 3:9, 10)**

Satan, as the "prince of darkness" and as the "prince of the powers of the air," is going to continually work on you with temptations, thoughts, and feelings that you do not like. However, the Word of God states,

> *"Neither yield ye your members as instruments*

---

41   The verb "to sin" in I John 3:9 is translated from the Greek word *hamartano*, which is a present active verb, implying or suggesting continued action.

of unrighteousness unto sin; but yield yourselves unto God... For sin shall not have dominion over you..." (Romans 6:12, 13)

"For though we walk in the flesh, we do not war after the flesh: (For the weapons of our warfare are not carnal but mighty through God to the pulling down of strongholds;) Casting down imaginations, and every high thing that exalts itself against the knowledge of God, and bringing into captivity every thought to the obedience of Christ..." (II Cor. 10:3-5)

WARRING AGAINST THE FLESH IN THE CHURCH

The sin question was dealt with above. The focus here is whether or not we understand what **a Spirit-led Church** is. Three and four generations ago, when most Americans had few skills, little education, and could not read, the people of God sought the Lord, enquired of God, and consulted God about everything. Today there has been a subtle but constant shift in the church's culture, purpose, and meaning. Today we have consultants, counselors, clubs, television, telephone, and the Internet. We rarely consult God about most decisions. Our **flesh**—that is, our emotions, desires, and will—"reviews" all our options prior to a decision, and perhaps never consults God.

For purposes of clarity, we need to review the meaning of **"the flesh"** in this context. We understand that the figurative term **"flesh"** refers to the physical existence of persons. We also recognize that Paul used the word to refer to **that part of man that can be controlled by sin and directed toward selfish pursuits.** In this section, the main purpose is to demonstrate how much **SELF (the flesh)** gets in the way of The Holy Ghost working miracles, signs, and wonders in our lives and in our churches. Above, the discussion was to enable the reader to see how the **sin-nature** can hinder if self and sin are not "crucified."

In this section, the discussion of **the flesh** is also geared toward the reader comprehending how **"self"** can plan, implement, and work in the church and on a church project without ever consulting God. (God of course is often asked to bless what He was not consulted about.) **Where the flesh operates and rules, God does not!** This section chapter aims to demonstrate how persons who operate according to their own ideas, designs, and wills without consulting God are really walking "*...according to course of this world...the spirit that now worketh in the **children of disobedience**, fulfilling the desires of **THE FLESH** and the mind...*" (Eph. 2:2, 3).

When any individual works very hard at fulfilling his/her own agenda or vision, and excludes seeking the Will of God, this indicates that the person is in a backslidden condition. *"The backslider in heart shall be filled with his own ways..."* (Prov. 14:14). It may be practical to distinguish between the **"backslider in heart,"** who remains active in the church, from **the backslider** who walks away from God and the church.

Charles Finney, the renowned 19th-century evangelist, offers this explanation for the **backslider in heart:**

The text [Prov. 14:14] *implies that there **may** be a backslidden heart, when the forms of religion and obedience to God are maintained. As we know from consciousness that men perform the same, or similar, acts from widely different, and often from opposite, motives, we are certain that we may keep up all the outward forms and appearance of religion, when in fact, they are backslidden in heart. No doubt the most intense selfishness often takes on a religious type, and are many considerations that might lead a backslider to keep up the forms, when he had lost the **power** of godliness in his soul."*[42] (author's emphasis)

Finney further expounds on the backslidden heart of the Christian:

–   Withdrawing oneself from a state of total devotion to God and coming again under the control of a self-pleasing spirit.

"Trust in the Lord with all thine heart; and lean not unto thine own understanding. In all thy ways acknowledge him, and he shall direct thy paths. Be not wise in thine own eyes..." (Prov. 3:5, 6, 7)

–   Taking back one's consecration to God and his service, forgetting...

---

42   From Charles Finney's book, *Revivals of Religion.* (CBN Univ. Press, Virginia Beach, VA), pp. 452, 3.

"When thou vowest a vow unto God, defer not to pay it; for he hath no pleasure in fools: pay that which thou hast vowed. Better it is that thou shouldest not vow, than that thou shouldest vow and not pay." (Eccl. 5:4, 5)

–   The Christian leaving their first love,[43] forgetting that Jesus said…

"So likewise, whosoever he be of you that forsaketh not all that he hath, he cannot be my disciple." **(Luke 14:33)**

The backslider in heart is the person who remains in church doing exactly what's in the heart to do. **Backsliding in heart is a gradual process**. The **backsliding-in-heart process** is a deceptively comfortable spiritual state, particularly for those persons who are faithful to church work. *"Let us search and try our ways, and TURN AGAIN TO THE LORD."* (Lam. 3:40)

–   Partially because of a lack of interest in God's Word.[44]

"Thy word have I hid in mine heart that I might not sin against thee." **(Psalm 119:11)**

–   Due to the failure to continuously sanctify oneself. All of us have ways of perceiving, thinking, and acting that are contrary to the Word of God and the Love of God. Some of this may be due to the **spirit of**

---

43   Ibid. pp. 452, 3.
44   See Appendix III for a Bible Study plan.

rejection, the spirit of pride, inferiority, etc. When we fail to work on these areas, as they are revealed to us by a sermon, a testimony, and/or God, we have allowed Satan a doorway to walk in with other oppressive spirits (Phil 4:8).

– If there is a lack of consistency in one's prayer life, which includes praise, intercession, "secret closet" seeking, etc. (Luke 18:1).

– If there is a lack of desire to reach the lost.

The Flesh and the Baby Saint

The new Christian, or "baby saint," touched by God and living on the "mountaintop," often becomes dissatisfied, worried, and frustrated when the "mountaintop feeling" subsides. This baby saint, not understanding, becomes anxious because the **feeling** is no longer there. Secondly, after the baby saint dwells on "why can't I continue feeling good," Satan is only too happy to poison this innocent person's mind, talking to them with the voice of their own mind and convincingly telling them, "You cannot be saved because God is not with you." This is the **flesh** desiring and seeking a **feeling** more than **the reality of serving** God.

After the new Christian has been saved and delivered—perhaps from drugs, violence, maybe even murder—God gives that person a powerful **testimony.** The people of God respond favorably with rejoicing to the extent that after the initial gratefulness of the new convert, **pride** begins to creep in. Further, the testimony will take on a new tone—perhaps a "spirit of boasting" and maybe exaggeration. The scripture *"neither give place to the devil..."* (Eph. 4:27) is a warning, even when testifying of freedom from past bondage and wickedness, because **the flesh** loves attention, particularly if a **spirit of rejection and/or inferiority** was part of that person's personal culture. **Pride** and a little bragging will enter, and a **doorway** to the past life of sin will be cracked open.[45] That spirit of the past life will be present and lurking, waiting for that doorway of pride to open, in order to walk back in with past torment and temptations.

EXAMPLE

In the late twenties in the Church of God in Christ, Bishop Charles Harrison Mason prayed for a woman who had a severe abscess in her lower jaw; she was in intense pain, and her whole jawbone was infected with the abscess. (In those times because of the deprivation of African Americans, there was a lack of health care and health insurance.) Immediately while she was being prayed for, the Holy Ghost operated on her jaw, and she spit out the infected jawbone. In addition, she was able to eat, and her face was not misshapen. (I do not know whether or not God performed a creation miracle and gave her a jawbone replacement.)

---

45 Satan will use anything to open a doorway to walk through or inject his oppressive demons back in the mind and spirit. Remember, the things that opened the doorway to Satan need not necessarily be related to the past. Satan just needs a slight change and he takes advantage.

Initially, her testimony was one of gratefulness and joy. The call for her testimony was so great, she soon began traveling and testifying with great pride and fanfare as though she herself had done the praying and the healing. Unfortunately, this woman loved all the attention and became so proud, she was cut off and, many feared, died in her sins.[46]

She (her FLESH) wanted attention, took personal credit for the miracles, and canceled the blessings of God for herself.

"I am the Lord: that is my name: and my glory will I not give another..." **(Isaiah 42:8)**

The Flesh and the Spiritually Ignorant

How often have you heard individuals saying, "The Lord told me to do..." or "The Lord showed me this about you..." or "The Lord is leading me to do..." Quite often, these persons may not be lying intentionally, but through that pervasive church demon, **spiritual ignorance,** some think that anything they think or feel in church is from the Holy Spirit. The bottom line is that God backs up and confirms His messages with results.

Bizarre behavior in services is either the person's **flesh (the desire to be seen),** or the devil in the person, or both. If a

---

46 Personal conversation with my father, Elder Ralph N. Ellis, who went to Memphis in 1922, was saved, filled with the Holy Ghost, and called to the ministry under Bishop Mason. My father served in his church until 1936.

person has to run all the way from the back of the church to begin praising the Lord in the front of the church, that is the flesh wanting attention. When you ask these persons why, inevitably, the response is **"God told me to do it."**

A worse scenario is the behavior during altar services that aids Satan in snatching "righteous Seed" being sown. How commonplace we find "altar-working busybodies" effectively hindering persons, telling them to call Jesus when the person is trying to say "Yes" to the Lord. It seems that these presumptuous busybodies forget to enquire of the Lord who they should pray with and how to pray. In one fellowship service with a group of churches, an outrageous example of **spiritual ignorance,** coupled with **the flesh** ruling instead of **God,** occurred.

EXAMPLE

The minister made an altar call at the end of his message. A young woman, a visitor, came to the church that evening and responded to the altar call. One evangelist was talking with her; I was standing on the other side of her, quietly praying. Suddenly from nowhere, two busybodies (who obviously had not sought the Lord for guidance and direction), both evangelists, rushed over and began screaming at the woman, "The blood of Jesus" and "Give up, give up." The woman became confused and went back to her seat.

Following that, another "altar-working busybody," one of the pastors in the fellowship, went in the back where the woman sat down and SLAPPED

THE WOMAN IN HER FACE!!! He stated he saw a "demon" at that spot. He then told one of his missionaries to pray for this woman. This missionary, immediately upon receiving her orders, began **speaking in tongues** and laying hands all over the woman's head. The poor woman didn't understand anything that was going on and was trying to get her bag and coat to leave.

Needless to say **the flesh and ignorance** were doing effective work to support "the evil one" in hindering God's incorruptible seed from being planted in this woman's heart. The woman, who was a schoolteacher, came to the service looking for help and continued to say, "I am not crazy and I don't have demons. I was looking for help. My husband and his girlfriend are trying to kill me and take my house."

The Flesh and Inherited Positions

Each one of us recognizes the normal rights of inheritance. What is accepted as normal in the natural may be totally abnormal in God's church. Worldliness in the church today seems to be the norm; the church promotes individuals and installs pastors, administrators, and officers based on blood ties, just as in the secular arena. All too often at the demise of a spiritual leader, the succession is not based on God's selection, but on political correctness and/or on the desire **(the flesh)** of the powerbrokers of the church. And so the scripture "without a vision the people perish" becomes real because the "heir apparent" was not God's selection and probably was not even saved.

EXAMPLE

Quite a few years ago, a young man (considered a favorite son), whose pastor was quite favored with the administrators of that region, was given a small congregation. After he pastored a period of time, the congregation fell off and almost disappeared. **IN SPITE OF THIS,** this favorite son was given another larger congregation with a debt-free building. These two congregations were combined. Over the years, the members left, debt increased, and the church became almost spiritually decadent. He then managed to become pastor of another thriving, debt-free church, the third one (which he combined with what was left of the other two churches). And, again members left and debt increased; the church is now barely alive.

The above demonstrates how arbitrary decisions (those made without consulting God) preface spiritual failure and harm to the household of faith.

The Flesh and Traditions of Men

> *"Beware lest any spoil you through philosophy and vain deceit, after the traditions of men not after Christ."* (Colossians 2:8)

Tradition means a body of unwritten religious precepts, any time-honored practice or set of practices, a mode of thought or behavior followed by a people continuously from generation to generation. Generally, religious traditions are the most difficult to change because every church has the same claim that their tenets, doctrine, and traditions are ordained of God. Notice for example, how denominations that have a strong foundation in the anointing of the Holy Ghost and being **spirit-led** seem to be able to maintain control of the majority of the followers through the continued ideology of the spirit-led leader. This means that whether the leader is spirit-led or not, because of powerful traditions, the population will follow and submit.

Generally, certain individuals often attempt to intimidate members by invoking supernatural sanctions. So the familiar scriptures are quoted to control people. *"Obey them that rule over you..."* **(Hebrews 13:17)**. But the remainder of that verse is not quoted as often with this phrase: *"...for they watch for your souls as they must give account, that they may do it with joy, and not with grief: for that is unprofitable for you."*

When new church leaders who are not consecrated continue to have the same authority as former church leaders who were consecrated, many insidious and damaging things happen:

1. Authority is abused, and leaders will often utilize their authority for self-serving gain, while advocating the ideology of **the spirit-led church**.

2. Scripture will still be preached and quoted, but great distortions will appear. *"The laborer is worthy of its hire"* is a favorite. You will notice that it is an

unwritten but powerful law that certain persons with certain titles must receive a minimum honorarium whether these persons deserve it or not and whether the persons giving it can afford to give or not.

When the traditions of men seem to rule more than the Spirit of God, the sacrifices of God are often ignored.

"THE SACRIFICES OF GOD are a broken spirit: A broken and a contrite heart, O God, thou wilt not despise." **(Psalm 51:17-19)**

"I beseech you therefore brethren, by the mercies of God, that you PRESENT YOUR BODIES A LIVING SACRIFICE, holy, acceptable under God, WHICH IS YOUR REASONABLE SERVICE." **(Romans 12:1)**

"By him therefore let us offer THE SACRIFICE OF PRAISE to God continually..." **(Hebrews 13:15)**

"BUT TO DO GOOD and to communicate forget not: for with such SACRIFICES God is well pleased." **(Hebrews 13:16)**

Unfortunately, tradition becomes custom, and custom becomes law. When personal material sacrifices (giving money) are admired and honored, the unwritten law becomes that you must be seen giving.

"Take heed that ye do not your alms before men,

to be seen of them: otherwise ye have no reward of your Father which is in heaven. Therefore, when thou doest thine alms, do not sound a trumpet before thee, as the hypocrites do in the synagogues and in the streets, that they may have glory of men..." (Matthew 6:1, 2)

"Doing the right thing" becomes a serious constraining factor against consecration to God, if you want to go up in some organizations.

"Thus saith the Lord: Cursed be the man that trusteth in man, and maketh flesh his arm, and whose heart departeth from the Lord." (Jer. 17:5)

"For PROMOTION cometh neither from the east, nor from the west, nor from the south. But God is the judge: he putteth down one and setteth up another." (Ps. 75:6, 7)

3. Followers tend to become like their leaders. Leaders who consecrate, pray, and witness will have followers doing the same. Leaders who love money above else will have their followers stressing money too. (Since the love of money is the root of **ALL EVIL**, the love of money precipitates a lot of scandal right in the church. A considerable portion of church work will be fund-raisers, programs, banquets, anniversaries, bus outings, etc. Church work then becomes a substitute for kingdom work, which is "to rescue the perishing.") Worst of all, the church that loses its first love, which is pleasing God by winning souls,

loses its true identity and anointing and is no longer **a spirit-led church.**

4. Because the Holy Spirit does not manifest Himself as people would desire, methods used in services rely on psychological suggestion and emotional ventilation. Consequently, there is a great reliance on music to **make things happen.**

5. The clarion cry of the holiness churches two generations ago—**"IT'S HOLINESS OR HELL AND NOTHING IN BETWEEN"**—is rarely heard **today.**

The Flesh and the Gifted

Many gifted musicians, singers, and preachers get caught up in their ability to produce results and forget that **GOD GIVES GIFTS TO MEN.** Even though many of these persons start out saved, perhaps as children in the church, their **FLESH** (their desire for money and fame) supersedes God's will for them. Successful individuals sometimes forget that sanctifying oneself is a lifelong journey for all believers.

EXAMPLE

One young man was called and anointed by God to preach the Gospel in his teens. He was naturally gifted to preach anyhow, and also had great oratorical skills and a winning personality. Through his gift and anointing, he began winning many souls to Christ;

his popularity and income soared. Later there was a change in the content of his messages; more entertaining than convicting. I asked, "Doesn't the Lord ever give you a judgment message?" His response was "I cannot say everything and keep doors open to my ministry." His statement to me, one day in another conversation, was "Preaching is an art. I am going to study and perfect the art; I plan to be the greatest preacher of my time." His skill at preaching has improved, the doors continue to be open, but socially and spiritually he is experiencing serious problems. Further, even though he is handling the Word of God as a pastor and evangelist, he is **backslidden in his heart** because his **flesh** (desires) has dictated his behavior.

Worse yet, the innocent hearers are enthralled and lifted with this kind of gifted preaching without power. People are often emotionally stirred and temporarily "blessed" by this exciting preaching, but the preaching that builds faith to stand for God at any cost is not necessarily found in artful, erudite preaching.

"For we are the circumcision which worship God in the spirit and rejoice in Christ Jesus and have no confidence in the flesh." (Phil. 3:3)[47]

Furthermore, in churches all over the country, there are ministers who once had ministries given and controlled by Holy

---

47   Read Philippians 3:3-12 to see the depth of Paul's commitment to God rather than himself, counting his genealogy, education, and sacrifices but "dung" that he could be instrumental for Christ.

Spirit. These ministers may have had great gifts of preaching, healing, or prophecy, but are now operating successfully and profitably in self—**the flesh**.

When anyone is used of the Holy Ghost to minister to God's people, the person learns how the Holy Ghost works through and in him/her. If, because of failure to consecrate and to humble oneself (not taking any of God's glory), the Holy Ghost departs, that person **HAS ALREADY LEARNED AND REMEMBERS** the workings of the Holy Ghost.

Most times these ministers keep on working their show in the same manner. Only now these ex-anointed ministers will make things happen by manipulating the faith of the hearers. After a while, these ministers will come to believe in themselves more than God. When you review services they have been in, the harvest, if there is one, does not last. Usually, these persons can pack a church for a week and do very well raising money, but if permanent decisions for Christ indicate real success, then little was accomplished. God is faithful and just, and He will honor His Word to those hearers believing the Gospel.

EXAMPLE

One young man, a gifted preacher with the gift of prophecy operating in his life, went through a painful, precipitous divorce. He was so hurt, it is the writer's opinion that he could not forgive his wife, who initiated the action while he was away from home. He had been raised with all half sisters and brothers and apparently had not fully dealt with all of the scars of his childhood. His reaction to these traumas is an example of how any doorway opened to the enemy will be exploited by the enemy. The **spirit of unforgiveness** opened him up to the old **spirit of rejection** from childhood, which included some sexual abuse. The shift in his relationship with God was obvious; his temper was short, bordering on violence, and he became more and more selfish. He began perfecting the art of the church con-artist, perfecting the special offering lines. Yet this young man has continued speaking in tongue, prophesying, and slaying people in the spirit (knocking individuals out in the floor). What has also evolved is the **"greedy dog"** spirit in which he calls for $100.00 offering lines, $50.00 offering lines, etc. He is so wounded, he is not seeking God for healing but is operating according to what he wants and his ability—**HIS FLESH**; money, clothes, material things have become his God.

Our answer to this is found:

> *"Not every one that saith to me, Lord, Lord, shall enter into the kingdom of heaven; but he that doeth the will of my Father which is in heaven. Many will say to me in that day, Lord, Lord, have we not prophesied in thy name: and in thy name have cast out devils? and in thy name done many wonderful works? And then I will profess unto them, I never knew you: depart from me, ye that work iniquity."*
> **(Matt. 7: 21-23)**

In many churches, people with the spirit of a **con artist** (the innate ability to manipulate emotions) will be put up to receive offerings. **These persons are gifted showpersons who know how to stimulate emotions (not faith) in order to receive large sums of money from the audience.** This is <u>spiritual whoredom</u> because all too often more effort is made to **invite** the Spirit of God in <u>during the offering</u> than at any other time during the service. This **seducing spirit** is so damaging because it makes people (even when they have not paid tithes) believe they can bribe God for blessings and favor.

> *"Yea, they are greedy dogs which can never have enough, and they are shepherds that cannot understand: they all look to their own way, every one for his gain, from his quarter."* (Isaiah 56:11)

<u>WHAT I MUST REALIZE!!!</u>

In your church and my church, Satan will use persons with great oratorical skills and will amplify their gifts. Notice the great proliferation of gifted adulterers, fornicators, homosexuals, and lesbians ministering at every level of the church. **THIS IS A POWERFUL WORK OF SATAN.**

> *"And I saw three unclean spirits like frogs come out of the mouth of the dragon, and out of the mouth of the beast, and out of the mouth of the false prophet."* (Rev. 16:13)

As the above scripture suggests, unclean spirits do come out of the mouths of unclean persons speaking (or praying). It is correct to conclude that fornicators, homosexuals, adulterers, liars, robbers, con artists minister their unclean spirits over God's people. Any hearers having similar areas of vulnerability will be affected by the spirit of that person ministering. On one occasion, I took an ex-felon (former drug dealer), a new convert, to a large church conference. When one preacher came to the podium and began speaking, this new convert said, "Why is that man up there? He is a con artist. I dealt with men like that in the street." In these perilous times, individuals need to be conscious that everyone preaching and praying or prophesying is not necessarily of God even though he/she may be handling the Word of God. It is interesting that sometimes baby saints can recognize hidden wickedness before the seasoned saint.

There are certain factors that suggest these messengers, their message, and/or their prophecies may be self-inspired or satanically inspired.

- Does the message build the Kingdom of God instead of man's kingdom and wealth (II Cor. 4:5)?

- What is the spiritual quality? Does it edify? Does it point to God? Is it disruptive (I Cor. 14:3, 33)?

- Does the prophecy **ALWAYS** come to pass (Deut.18:22)? (Most of us can become good at "hit or miss" prophecies.)

- Are they usually prophecies that the Bible promises anyhow? For example, "If thou wouldest praise me,

I will be in the midst thee, thus saith the Lord thy God." The Psalmist wrote this a few thousand years ago; Psalms 22:3. Furthermore, God is quite capable of speaking in 20th century American (colloquial) English.

Even if the message appears godly and is the truth, it can be from Satan. Recall the women in The Acts of the Apostles with the spirit of divination who continuously followed Paul, saying; *"These men are the servants of the most High God, which shew unto us the way of Salvation"* (Acts 16:17). Satan is so subtle in working with man with what is familiar to him, individuals will not recognize when his **own sin nature** is ruling. Satan will assist the believer into "sliding into a comfort zone" in the church and help him/her to operate in the flesh.

Men and women everywhere must never forget that being made in the image of God means that each person is given intelligence and a will that the individual uses every day for all aspects of life. The will of man, his decision-making power, is what determines relationship with God.

Being a WARRIOR is not an option,

but a MANDATE from GOD!

"Ye are of God little children, and have overcome them, for greater is He that is in you than he that is in the world." (I John 4:4)

WARRIORS: PREPARED, FIGHTING, AND WINNING

"Finally, my brethren, BE STRONG IN THE LORD, and in the POWER OF HIS MIGHT." (Eph. 6:10)

This is a command, not a suggestion or request! The believer must receive this Power, that is, have this Power working and abiding in his life on a daily basis. Inasmuch as there are no exact translations from any one language to another, carefully examine all of the hidden information in this scripture. The word *strong* derives from the Greek word *endunamoo,* which means to empower or make strong, with the prefix *en* meaning *into.* This phrase, *"be strong in the Lord"* in the immediate imperative indicates that you must allow God's supernatural Power to be actively working you.

Notice that the word *power* in Acts 1:8 (*"But ye shall receive Power..."*) has the same root word and thus a similar meaning, *ability, abundance, but specifically miraculous power.* The word *power* in the second portion of this scripture ("...

in the POWER of his might") has a different meaning than the word *power* used in Acts 1:8. The word in this scripture derives from the word *kratos,* which means *might, force, strength,* especially *manifested power.* But this word also is used to translate *dominion. Dominion* refers to *sovereignty* or *exercising control or rule in a territory or sphere of influence.*

THE PRECONDITIONS AND PREPARATION

Therefore, the command for the believer is to get ready and stay ready and to be filled, infused, saturated with the Power of God to **OCCUPY UNTIL THE LORD RETURNS.** In other words, allow Satan no ground in your mind, in your behavior, in your family, in your church. You must keep the enemy defeated! As in any discipline, profession, or craft, there are prerequisites and preconditions for an initial point of entry. Thus, the preconditions for **warriors** to be invested with God's Power are:

The Fear of God

The **fear of God** has nothing to do with horror, dread, or intimidation, but rather it is a **reverential fear. Reverential fear** means that the individual has a wholesome fear or dread of displeasing the awesomely powerful GOD OF THE UNIVERSE. **The Fear of God** becomes the controlling motive for the individual's life: *"By the fear of the Lord men DEPART FROM EVIL"* (Prov. 16:6).

The fear that most of us are accustomed to recognizing is *"the spirit of bondage to fear"* (Romans 8:15). Fear that causes bondage makes persons withdraw, hide, fight, or flee. In other words, the fear that Satan sends is a first cousin to terror, and terror paralyzes positive action. On the other hand, **reverential fear** carries powerful but eternal benefits...

Blessings: *"Blessed is the man that feareth the Lord, that delighteth greatly in his commandments"* (Psalm 112:1).

Peace: *"What man is he that feareth the Lord...? His soul shall dwell at ease..."* (Psalm 25:12, 13). *"Happy is the man that feareth always..."* (Prov.28:14).

Wisdom: *"The fear of the Lord is instruction and wisdom..."* (Prov. 15:33). *"The fear of the Lord is the beginning of knowledge..."* (Prov. 1:7).

Fear is learned behavior, whether it is fear of people, places, or things. Similarly, *reverential fear of God* must be learned, and there is no better place to start than with the Bible.

God is the GOD OF THE EVERYWHERE: *"For the eyes of the Lord run to and fro throughout the whole earth, to shew himself strong in the behalf of them whose heart is perfect toward him..."* (**II Chron. 16:9**)

God is the GOD OF JUDGEMENT AND JUSTICE: *"God shall bring every work into judgment, with every secret thing, whether it be good, or whether it be evil"* (**Eccl. 12:14**). *"The soul that sinneth* *shall die. The son shall not bear the iniquity of the Father, neither shall the father bear the iniquity of the son: the righteousness of the righteous shall be upon him, and the wickedness of the wicked shall be upon him"* **(Ezekiel 18:20).**

Also know that God, whose "mercy endureth forever,"[48] is the same God who states, emphatically, *"vengeance belongeth to me…"* (Hebrews 10:30).

"Ah Lord God! behold thou hast made the heaven and the earth by thy great power and stretched out arm, and there is nothing too hard for thee: Great in counsel, and mighty in work: for thine eyes are open upon all the ways of the sons of men: to give every one according to his ways and according to the fruit of his doings." **(Jer. 32:17, 19)**

The *fear of the Lord* must be taught, inculcated, and cultivated in the lives of every believer. Saved and unsaved alike can recognize God in the dawn, the blade of grass, the bee making honey, the laughter of a tot, but also in the floods of '93 and hurricanes Hugo of '91 and Andrew of '92. The **warrior** must learn to see God in the awesome wonders of nature as well as in times of trials, knowing that there is nothing TOO HARD FOR GOD (Jer. 32:27).

"Gather the people together, men, and women, and children, and thy stranger that is within thy gates, that they may hear, and that they may learn, and

---

48   Written over thirty times in the Bible.

fear the Lord your God and observe to all the words of this law." (Deut. 31:12)

Love for God

Love can never be defined in its fullest sense. However, love can be observed, demonstrated, and felt. Since *"…God is Love…"* (I John 4:16), God freely gives man His Love (John 3:16; Ro. 5:8; Jer. 31:3). Therefore, it is not difficult to give God our best in love.

"And thou shall love the Lord thy God with all thy heart and with all thy soul, and with all thy mind, and with all thy strength …" (Mark 12:30)

We are not ready to be **warriors** if the results of God's love in us (the "Fruit of the Spirit")[49] cannot be observed along with our sharing and helping the household of faith (John 13:35, Gal. 6:10). Jesus said, *"If ye love me keep my commandments… He that hath my commandments and keepeth them, he it is that loveth me: and he that loveth me shall BE LOVED OF MY FATHER and I will love him, and will manifest myself to him* (John 14:15, 21). Certainly if we cannot conquer "the lack of Love," surely we will fail when warring against Satan. However, the Word assures of power for the warfare as well as His Love (II Tim. 1:7).

"Herein is our love made perfect… THERE IS NO FEAR IN LOVE, but perfect LOVE CASTS OUT FEAR: because fear hath torment. He that feareth

---

49   Galatians 5:22, 23.

is not made perfect in love." (I John 4:17a, 18).

Obedience: Salvation and Sanctification

Obedience to anything is contrary to the **sin nature** of man.[50]

Obedience, in its strictest sense, is submission to the control and commands of another. Jesus said, *"...If any man will come after me, let him deny himself, and take up his cross daily, and follow me"* (Luke 9:23). Sanctification is included in this scripture.[51] Self-denial must include all weights (which includes, but is not limited to, all TV addiction like the soaps, boxing, baseball, football, X-rated movies, etc.), Internet addictions like Facebook and Twitter, and sins (fornicating, lying, failure to tithe properly, backbiting, gossiping, slothfulness). None of us are perfect, and sometimes the sanctification process becomes bumpy and we do not always make a hundred. However, the Word of God pointedly instructs, *"My little children, these things write I unto you, that ye sin not, And if any man sin, we have an advocate with the Father, Jesus Christ, the righteous..."* Therefore *"If we confess our sins, he is faithful and just to forgive us our sins, and to cleanse us from all unrighteousness"* (I John 2:9).

Confession is only the first step. After confessing you must recognize or identify those areas in which you have problems. Then you must work on yourself. Jesus will never do for you what you can do for yourself: *"...Let us CLEANSE*

---

50   See chapter called "The Sin Nature/Flesh."
51   Read the chapter "Sanctification, a Lifetime Process" in *Called to Be Saints*, by Fay Ellis Butler.

OURSELVES from all filthiness of the flesh and spirit, perfecting holiness in the fear of God..." (II Cor. 7:1). Perfecting holiness also includes separation (which is sometimes painful spiritual surgery) as well as sanctification; there are friends and acquaintances, perhaps even a job that must be let go. Whatever it takes for the Power of God to operate in the Christian's life, Christians willing to war against Satan must do it.

> *"I have been crucified with Christ; nevertheless I live; yet not I but Christ liveth in me; and life which I now live in the flesh I live by FAITH IN THE SON OF GOD, who loved me and gave himself for me."*
> **(Gal. 2:20)**

When any individual has repented and allowed **the Blood of Jesus** to wash his/her sins away, he/she is, in the sight of God, legally and spiritually crucified with Christ (Gal. 2:20). Therefore, relationally, you are ONE with Him (Romans 8:17) and dead to sin (Romans 6:5-7). But Paul acknowledges that we must live in the flesh, not on our own, but *"...by the Faith of the Son of God..."* Our crucifixion marks the death of our old sinful nature, while the resurrection gives us the Power to defeat the enemy in every area of our lives. As the Christian is faithful to the Word continuously and progressively (not repenting for the same things over and over), God will trust him/her with more and more of **His Anointing.**

> *"He hath showed thee, O man, what is good; and what doth the Lord require of thee, but to do justly, and to love mercy, and walk humbly with thy God?"*
> **(Micah 6:8)**

Humility

Humility is lowliness, meekness, mildness, modesty, and submissiveness. Spiritually, humility is the quality in a Christian that recognizes that our worth comes from God alone. The Bible instructs, *"Let us not be desirous of vain glory"* (Gal. 5:26), or in other words, unwarranted celebration of one's accomplishments or qualities. Remember, all good gifts and perfect gifts come from God (James 1:17) and also that God rains on the just as well as the unjust (Matt. 5:45). Whether a person is saved or unsaved, God should be honored for all blessings and gifts.

When it comes to working in and for God's kingdom, we **WORK WITH GOD'S POWER** according to His direction. The more faithful we are to the labor He has called us to, and the more glory we give to Him, the more He **lifts us up.** No person in or of themselves can save, heal, or deliver; only the Holy Spirit does the Work of God through the worthy, humble individual.

> *"...Clothe yourselves with humility toward one another because 'God opposes the proud but GIVES GRACE TO THE HUMBLE.' Humble yourselves, therefore, under God's mighty hand, that He may lift you up in due time."* (I Peter 5:5, 6)

As was discussed above in the section entitled "The Sin Nature," it is natural for man to be self-centered and proud. Therefore when the Word states, *"...Clothe yourselves with humility..."* it is referring to the Christian exercising his/her will. **In other words, the Christian working for God**

must make a continuous conscious effort to ascribe one's achievement to God and to always give others credit for their labors. Notice the word *clothe* derives from the Greek word *egkomboomai,* which means to attach a piece of clothing to oneself. In New Testament times, slaves had to fasten a white piece of cloth or apron over their clothing so that their slave status would be recognized.

First of all, believers clothed in humility believe clothing their behavior in humility will identify them as being Christlike. Secondly, as God is given the honor and glory, He gives the humble person more of His Grace, *"...but gives GRACE to the humble..."* Thirdly, being exalted or lifted up by God is a spiritual elevation. It should follow that if the Christian humbles him/herself (spiritual submission) under God's mighty hand, that God is the One who exalts (greater spiritual blessings and anointing will surely come).

This indicates that the Biblical concept of an individual being exalted has nothing to do with appointments or positions given by men. *The Fear of God, The Love of God, Obedience, Sanctification, and Humility* are preconditions or prerequisites for the power of God to be invested in the Christian (for war).

Preparation for War

In the armed services, there are basic rudimentary skills that all recruits must have. Boot training is necessary before specialization, whether it is the Air Force pilots, Navy SEALs, Green Berets, paratroopers, radiomen, weapons specialists, or Army engineers. Anyone entering the armed services

MUST HAVE BASIC SKILLS.

As stated in the Introduction, as soon as a person accepts the Lord as his/her personal savior, he/she is "a new creation" and then he/she becomes a target for Satan. Whatever the sins of the past (prior to salvation), the demons controlling those sins will follow the "babe in Christ." *"For whatsoever is born of God overcometh the world: and this is the victory that overcometh the world, even our faith"* **(I John 5:4).** However, faith must be cultivated, nourished, and built up.

Studying and Memorizing the Word of God

The faith that overcomes the world is the faith that is built up daily in the Word. *"So then faith cometh by hearing, and hearing by the Word of God"* (Romans 10:17).

The Word of God is heard and discussed in Sunday School; ATTENDING SUNDAY SCHOOL BUILDS FAITH.

The Word of God is taught and explained in Bible Study; ATTENDING BIBLE STUDY BUILDS FAITH.

The Word of God is preached and taught by the pastor and the ministerial staff. The Word is heard in testimony in regular church services; ATTENDING CHURCH SERVICES BUILDS FAITH.

In addition to hearing the Word, the Word must be studied and memorized. The Word gives "a settled peace" in troubled times: *"Great peace have they which love thy law: and nothing shall offend them"* (Psalm 119:165). The memorized

Word will help the believer stay saved: *"Thy Word have I HID IN MY HEART that I might not sin against thee"* (Psalm 119:11). The memorized Word is a weapon against the enemy.

Fasting

Part of the basics includes FASTING. Fasting is abstinence from nourishment, food, and/or drink. However, in these polluted times of a polluted entertainment media, believers sometimes need to fast from most of the entertainment that comes on the television and definitely fast from long, frivolous phone conversations as well as the social network (Facebook and Twitter). Fasting helps in crucifying self (Psalm 35:13, Ps 69:10).

Praying

Faith is built also by praying in the Spirit. There are different types of prayer: intercession, praise, petition, thanksgiving, travail, meditation, etc. Every believer must cultivate a spirit of prayer because *"Men ought to always pray and not to faint"* (Luke 18:1). Satan may send the temptations, trials, and tribulations, but a consistent prayer life will give power to resist the devil. Therefore, Satan will not be able to inject thoughts and spirits of rejection, rage, inferiority, lust, and slothfulness into the mind and spirit of the prayerful believer.

God does not go on vacation. God, the self-existent ONE, does not get tired, and He NEVER slumbers nor sleeps (Psalm 121:4). Therefore, when the Word enjoins, *"Continue in prayer..."* (Col. 4:2) several messages should be heard.

First, God is an ever present Savior, Friend, and Deliverer (Psalm 46:1). The second fact is if you are steadfast in prayer, you should have the assurance that the answer is on the way.

"And this is the confidence that we have in him, that if we ask any thing according to his will, he heareth us: And if we know that he hear us, WHATSOEVER WE ASK, WE KNOW THAT WE HAVE the petitions that we desired of HIM." (I John 5:14, 15)

Get the fact of His willingness to give you a hearing in your mind and spirit. Memorize Hebrews 4:14-16:

Seeing then, that we have a GREAT HIGH PRIEST that is passed into the heavens, JESUS THE SON OF GOD, let us hold fast our profession. For we have not an high priest which cannot be touched with the feeling of our infirmities; but was in ALL POINTS tempted like as we are, yet WITHOUT SIN. Let us, therefore, COME BOLDLY unto the Throne of Grace to find help in the time of need." (Hebrews 4:14-16)

Thirdly, *"...continue in prayer..."* very strongly mandates self-discipline, especially since the balance of that verse reads *"...and watch in the same with thanksgiving..."* The hidden meaning seems to suggest that the weakness of our human nature would cause a neglect of prayer. Our safety, protection, healing, and peace are dependent on our prayer life.

Furthermore, prayer is the ONLY METHOD BY

WHICH GOD CAN HEAR FROM YOU. No one can go to God for you like you can pray to God for yourself.

Your help is **a prayer away.** There are no special formulas for prayer, except Jesus taught men to pray in a manner similar to the Lord's prayer; included should be worship, surrender to God's Will, petition, repentance, forgiveness, and closing with praise. However, Jesus also commanded that we pray to the Father in His Name. Therefore, when we pray, we call to our Father, IN THE NAME OF JESUS: *"... ye shall ask the Father in my name..."* (John 14:13, 15:16; 16:23, 26).

Asking **IN JESUS' NAME** indicates that your prayer is in accord with Jesus' Will and His Character.

Asking **IN HIS NAME** also carries with it a spirit of submission and humility.

Asking **IN HIS NAME** immediately gets the Father's attention because the Father recognizes His Son's Blood applied to your life.

Since the Holy Spirit abides (dwells) in the believer's spirit, as the believer prays, the Holy Spirit will interpret the needs of your human heart (to the Father) even when *"...we know not what we should pray for as we ought..."* (Romans 8:26, 27).

- Sometimes you must get alone and pray, but **PRAY** (Matt. 6:6).

- Sometimes you may need to pray all night, **but PRAY** (Luke 6:12).

- Sometimes it is necessary to FAST and pray, **but PRAY** (Dan. 9:3).

- Sometimes it is necessary to have a special time to meet God, **but PRAY** (Psalm 55:17; Acts 10:9).

- Sometimes it is necessary for the church to set aside a special time of seeking, **but PRAY** (Joel 1:13, 14; Acts 12:5).

You can pray bowing (Ex. 4:31); kneeling (Eph. 3:14); on your face (Joshua 5:14); standing (Luke 18:11); or just going about your activities of daily living, but PRAY. **BASIC TRAINING WITHOUT PRAYER IS NO TRAINING AT ALL.**

"PRAYING ALWAYS WITH ALL PRAYER and supplication in the Spirit, and watching thereunto with all perseverance and supplication for all saints." **(Eph. 6:18)**

Witnessing

"But ye shall receive power, after that the Holy Ghost is come upon you: and ye shall be WITNESSES UNTO ME both in Jerusalem, and in all Judea, and in Samaria and unto the uttermost part of the earth." **(Acts 1:8)**

The Holy Ghost empowers every believer to witness. This empowerment gives the believer the ability to bring in a harvest. As you give out of yourself with witnessing, praying, serving, the Lord adds more power to your life. In essence, you may lose what you have if you don't use what you have been given. Witness to children, your relatives, friends, and coworkers. You don't have to be deep, brilliant, or erudite; just say like the Psalmist, *"Come and hear, all ye that fear God and I will declare what he hath done for my soul" (Psalm 66:16).*

There are, admittedly, times when you feel as though you should witness, but the opportunity does not present itself. Every Christian, therefore, should carry a small assortment of appropriate tracts. Tracts are called the "silent evangelists." You don't have to be in "the tract ministry," but you can give out a tract from time to time as a consistent witness for God.

"But sanctify the Lord God in your hearts: and be ready always to give an answer to every man that asketh for a reason of the hope that is in you, with meekness and fear." (I Peter 3:15)

THE WEAPONS OF OUR WARFARE

War maims, kills, destroys. When the enemy comes with massive weapons of destruction, missiles, tanks, howitzers, machine guns, **he must be stopped!!!** A peashooter is inappropriate. Similarly, Satan is using massive, multiple evil powers of darkness, whether it is new ideologies (like the New Age Movement), or the malicious molding of young minds through the television, or blatant witchcraft, Satanism, and the Neo-Nazi movements. These exist and affect your life, the lives of your loved ones, and even churches, whether this evil is recognized or not. Do you, for example, know whether or not your child's teacher is a Satanist? Is your doctor a wizard or witch? Does the grocery store on the corner market certain items for witchcraft, or do you walk in the presence of witchcraft because palm reading is going on in the back of your local candy store?

As discussed in previous chapters, the churches and our families are not exempt. The Battle was fought and won at Calvary and the Resurrection. However, Satan doesn't stop. Therefore, God gave us weapons to keep him defeated. Consider these weapons like atomic warfare; they destroy everything in their path. They are:

THE WORD OF GOD

THE NAME OF JESUS

THE BLOOD OF JESUS

THE HOLY GHOST

PRAISE AND WORSHIP

SPEAKING IN OTHER TONGUES

The Word of God as a WEAPON OF WARFARE

The **Word of God** has always been a weapon of war; even in the Bible itself, the Word of God is metaphorically described as a weapon or tool of power.

"The Word of God is quick and POWERFUL, and SHARPER THAN ANY TWO EDGED SWORD, piercing even to the dividing asunder of soul and spirit, and of the joints and marrow, and is a <u>discerner of the thoughts and intents of the heart.</u>" (Hebrews 4:12)

"And take the helmet of salvation, and the SWORD OF THE SPIRIT, which is the WORD OF GOD." (Eph. 6:17)

"Is not MY WORD like as a fire? saith the Lord; and like a HAMMER that breaketh a rock to pieces?" (Jer. 23:29)

Understand that if you have received Jesus, you have received the **PERSONAL AND PERSONIFIED WORD OF GOD.**

"In the beginning was the Word, and the Word was with God, and the Word was God... And the Word was made flesh, and dwelt among us... As many as received him, to them gave he power to become the sons of God, even to them that believe on his name." (John 1:1, 14, 10)

Jesus as **THE WORD** revealed the heart and mind of God. Further, as **THE WORD**, He demonstrated His own pre-existent power as recorded in Genesis, *"In the beginning GOD..."*

"God, who in sundry times and in divers manners

spoke in time past unto the fathers by the prophets, hath in these last days spoken unto us by his Son, whom he hath appointed heir of all things, by whom also he made the worlds..." (Hebrews 1:1, 2)

Verifying the power in the Word of God, Jesus used the Word of God to defeat the enemy. Jesus responded to Satan's temptation in the wilderness during his forty-day fast with the Word of God:

"It is written, man not shall live by bread alone..."

"It is written again, thou shalt not tempt the Lord thy God..."

"Get thee hence, Satan: for it is written, thou shalt worship the Lord thy God, and him only shalt thou serve." (Matt. 4:3-11)

Then the scripture states, *"THEN THE DEVIL LEAVETH HIM..."* (Matt. 4:11).

He used **HIS WORD** to deliver: *"...he cast out spirits with "HIS WORD..."* (Matt. 8:16). In the Psalms you will also find, *"He SENT HIS WORD and healed them and delivered them from destructions* (Psalm 107:20).

As powerful as the Word of God is, it will be ineffective if you do not know and understand your powerful rights in the Word of God. Therefore,

GET IN THE WORD: *"Seek ye out of the BOOK OF THE*

LORD, and read: no one of these shall fail..." (Isaiah 34:16).

LIVE BY THE WORD: *"THY WORDS were found and I did eat them; and THY WORD was unto me the joy and rejoicing of mine heart..."* (Jer. 15:16). *"Now ye are clean through THE WORD which I have spoken unto you"* (John 15:3).

ALLOW THE WORD TO GUIDE YOU: *"THY WORD is a lamp unto my feet, and a light unto my path"* (Psalm 119:105).

ALLOW THE WORD OF GOD TO BUILD YOU UP: *"And now brethren, I commend you to God, and the WORD OF HIS GRACE, which is able to build you up and give you an inheritance among all them which are sanctified"* (Acts 20:32).

Every believer has the right and the duty to become powerful in the Word of God, but commitment means WORK.

WORK AT STUDYING THE WORD: *"These were more noble than those in Thessalonica, in that they received THE WORD with all readiness of mind, and SEARCHED THE SCRIPTURES daily, whether those things were so"* (Acts 17:11).

WORK AT MEDITATING ON THE WORD: *"Oh, how I love YOUR LAW! It is my meditation all day..."* (Psalm 119:97).

WORK AT MEMORIZING THE WORD: *"Therefore ye shall lay up these MY WORDS in your heart, and in your soul…"* (Deut. 11:18). *"THY WORD have I hid in my heart that I might not sin against thee"* (Psalm 119:11).

Further, ATTEND SUNDAY SCHOOL AND BIBLE STUDY.

Consider the Word of God as the source of your spiritual life. Spiritual life cannot be sustained without the Word. Moreover, the Word of God used by the believer is a powerful **"demon-busting" too**l. When you pray or testify to what the Word states, you are reminding Satan that he has already been defeated. Further, as you use the Word in spiritual warfare, it increases your confidence as you see the results. Why, for example, does the Word state, *"Death and life are in the power of the tongue: and they that love it shall eat the fruit thereof" (Prov. 18:21)*? Whatever you speak is heard by you, because your will is involved in your utterances— these words enter your spirit. Based on that principle alone, the Word is a weapon against the enemy's attacks against you because the Lord said *"…I will hasten MY WORD to perform it…"* (Jer. 1:12).

Use the Word to defeat Satan's demonic attacks!!!

FOR INFERIORITY AND LOW SELF-ESTEEM: *"I can do all things THROUGH CHRIST which strengtheneth me"* (Phil 4:13).

FOR MENTAL TORMENT AND INSANITY: *"…he was bruised for our iniquities; the chastisement of our peace was upon him...*" (Isaiah 53:5). "*Thou wilt keep him in perfect peace, whose mind is stayed on thee...*" (Isaiah 26:3).

FOR RESTLESSNESS AND UNCERTAINTY: "*Let your conversation be without covetousness; and be content with such things as ye have for HE HATH SAID I WILL NEVER LEAVE THEE nor forsake thee. So that we may boldly say, the LORD IS MY HELPER...*" (Hebrews 13:5, 6).

FOR GUILT AND CONDEMNATION FROM ONE'S PAST: "*There is therefore now NO CONDEMNATION to them which are in Christ Jesus, who walk not after the flesh, but after the Spirit*" (Romans 8:1).

FOR THE DOMINION OF DRUGS, LUST, AND ALCOHOL: "*The Law of the Spirit of Life hath set me free from the law of sin and death*" (Romans 8:2).

FOR FEAR: "*For God hath not given us the spirit of fear; but of power, and of love and of a sound mind*" (II Tim. 1:7).

FOR THE INABILITY TO LEARN: "*If any of you lack wisdom, let him ask of God, that giveth to all men liberally, and upbraideth not; and it shall be given him*" (James 1:5).

FOR SPIRITUAL IGNORANCE: "*But of him are ye in Christ, who OF GOD IS MADE UNTO WISDOM, and righteousness*" (I Cor. 1:30).

FOR UNBELIEF: *"…God hath dealt to every man a measure of faith…"* (Romans 12:3).

FOR SPIRITUAL DEFEAT: *"Ye are of God, little children, and have OVERCOME THEM: because GREATER IS HE that is in you than he that is in the world"* (I John 4:4). *"Now thanks be to God, which ALWAYS CAUSES US TO TRIUMPH IN CHRIST"* (II Cor. 2:14).

FOR SICKNESS: *"…With HIS STRIPES WE ARE HEALED…"* (Isaiah 53:5).

FOR ANY AND ALL ANXIETY: *"Casting ALL YOUR CARE UPON HIM; for he careth for you"* (I Peter 5:7).

The Word not only has the answer but will bring deliverance. Use the Word of God freely; substitute your name for any pronoun in each scripture. Watch God *"hasten to perform his Word."*

EXAMPLE

I was able to deal with one woman who was possessed by the devil, who spoke with the voice of a demon and said, "I didn't stay in the swine." We know from the Bible story that the man of Gadara called himself Legion, "for we are many." A legion in Bible times was around 6,000. For over four hours, every voice and lie the demons spoke, the Lord gave me a scripture to demolish the lie and that demon. Eventually the woman was able to repent and ask the Lord to forgive her rebellion because she hated God.

After that, the rest of the deliverance was easy. Note it was THE WORD OF GOD that defeated all the demons and forces of darkness.

The Name of JESUS as a WEAPON OF WARFARE

First of all the Name "Jesus" means, literally, DELIVERER or SAVIOR. Secondly, Jesus, the Son of God, is preeminent in time and in eternity:

> *"But to us there is but one God, The Father, of whom ARE ALL THINGS, and we are in him; and one Lord Jesus Christ, by WHOM ARE ALL THINGS, and we by Him."* **(I Cor. 8:6)**

> *"And Jesus came and spoke unto them, saying ALL POWER IS GIVEN UNTO ME IN HEAVEN AND IN EARTH."* **(Matt. 28:18)**

> *"...I am Alpha and Omega..."* **(Rev. 1:11)**

First of all, repenting and calling on the Name of Jesus saves us from sin (Romans 10:13). Then Jesus gave us authority and power because we accepted Him: *"Behold, I give unto you POWER to tread on serpents and scorpions and over all the power of the enemy..."* **(Luke 10:19; John 1:12).** The NAME OF JESUS is so awesomely great that His disciples were healing and casting out devils before they had received the Baptism of the Holy Ghost (Mark 9:38-39). We, therefore, pray TO THE FATHER IN THE NAME OF JESUS because:

- **HE is our Savior** (John 3:16).

- **HE is our High Priest and Intercessor** (Hebrews 4:16).

- **HE is our Advocate with the Father** (I John 2:1).

- **HE is our Healer** (Is. 53:5; I Pe. 2:24).

Therefore, when we pray IN THE NAME OF JESUS, we are simply agreeing with what He said He would do.

When the believer stands and uses the Name of Jesus, he or she is:

1) Representing the righteousness of God (II Cor. 5:21); and

2) Working or standing in Jesus' shoes (John 16:23, 24)— **"the power of attorney."** The miracle of healing as Peter spoke at the Gate called Beautiful, *"...such as I have give I unto thee, IN THE NAME OF JESUS CHRIST OF NAZARETH, rise up and walk"* **(Acts 3)**, is a demonstration of "standing in Jesus' stead." It is important to fully understand why the NAME OF JESUS is an awesome WEAPON OF WAR against the devil.

FACT 1: **The FATHER works IN THE NAME OF JESUS!!!**

Jesus said that you will have limitless power from the Father because you are working in His Name (John 15:16).

FACT 2: Jesus works IN HIS OWN NAME!!!

For the Glory of His Father, Jesus said He would do whatever was asked in His Name (John 14:13, 14).

FACT 3: Being saved is the only condition for using HIS NAME.

"And these signs SHALL follow them that believe…" The power to minister the Spirit of God is instantaneous when the believer prays:

> *"In MY NAME SHALL they cast out devils;*
>
> *they SHALL speak with new tongues;*
>
> *they SHALL take up serpents;*
>
> *and if they drink any deadly thing,*
>
> *it SHALL NOT hurt them*
>
> *they SHALL lay hands on the sick*
>
> *and they SHALL recover."* (Mark 16:17-18)

"SHALL" in this text speaks of inevitable, unconditional, powerful results as a believer prays **IN THE NAME OF JESUS.** Notice that *follow* in this scripture comes from the Greek word *parakoloutheo*, from *para*, meaning *beside*, and *koloutheo*, meaning *accompany*, or literally *accompanying side by side*. In other words, AS SOON AS YOU BEGIN

PRAYING TO THE **FATHER, IN THE NAME OF JESUS,** the POWER OF GOD is present to work!!!

EXAMPLE

A few years ago, I traveled to Sao Paolo, Brazil for a women's conference. The same day I arrived, after a nine-hour flight, I was called on to speak in the evening service. A man began barking like a dog, throwing a towel back and forth over his head, and moving from one side to another, really disrupting the service. To be perfectly honest, I was tired and a little more than annoyed. I did not feel any great anointing either. I walked over to the man and COMMANDED IN THE NAME OF JESUS, *"You foul spirit, come out of him now."* The man immediately stopped barking and moving around in the church, and I was informed he never did that again. It was the "power of attorney," representing Jesus, using His Name, which will work miracles.

The BLOOD of JESUS as a WEAPON OF WARFARE

First of all, the **Blood of Jesus** was central to the complete work of redemption: ***"...without shedding of Blood is no remission..."*** (Hebrews 9:22). Secondly, He, our Lord, Jesus Christ, has ransomed all believers from Satan's evil power:

> ***"And they sung a new song, saying, Thou art worthy to take the book, and to open the seals thereof:***

for thou was slain, and has redeemed us to God by thy BLOOD out of EVERY kindred, and tongue and people and nation." (Rev. 5:9)

Consequently, because of THE BLOOD OF JESUS received by believers, God gives His Spirit to the believers. If one understands that the Father recognizes the Son's BLOOD as soon as the believer prays IN THE NAME OF JESUS, one can likewise understand that Satan also recognizes THE BLOOD-WASHED saint. Therefore, when the believer "holds" the BLOOD OF JESUS against the assaults or the wiles of the devil, the devil must retreat.

"...For the accuser of our brethren is cast down, which accused them before God day and night. And they OVERCAME him by the BLOOD OF THE LAMB, and the word of their testimony; and they loved not their lives unto the death." (Rev. 12:10, 11)

The word *overcame* derives from the Greek word *nikao,* which means *the mightiest prevail.* Therefore, Satan may affect possessions, the physical body, and even one's relatives, but he cannot stop THE BLOOD-WASHED SAINT, whose mind is made up to serve Christ and defeat the devil. Satan becomes powerless in the presence of the people of God praying, *"LORD, LET YOUR BLOOD PREVAIL."*

The Holy Spirit as a WEAPON OF WARFARE

The HOLY SPIRIT has many operations. As the executive agent of the Trinity, He brings about the will of the Father and the Son in the earth. He, the Holy Spirit, works in and with the believer to fulfill the Will of the Father and the Son.

- **HE** brings salvation; John 3:5-8.

- **HE** sanctifies; Romans 15:16; II Thessalonians 2:13.

- **HE** teaches, comfort, guides; John 14:26; I John 2:27.

- **HE** delivers; Mark 16:16, 17.

- **HE** baptizes and fills the saints; Acts 2:4.

- **HE** baptizes believers into the Body of Christ; I Corinthians 12:13.

- **HE** is the POWER that defeats all the power of the enemy; Luke 10:19.

The Holy Ghost is so powerful; He is like a secret weapon. Notice the Holy Ghost actively and visibly works in and for you, but it is marvelously overwhelming when you realize that the Holy Ghost will work for you even when you are unaware.

"When the enemy shall come in like a flood, THE SPIRIT OF THE LORD <u>SHALL</u> LIFT UP a standard against him." **(Isaiah 59:19)**

The STANDARD in ancient warfare was like a country's flag today. The STANDARD was always present in the front of the fighting forces; as long as the enemy saw the STANDARD coming toward them, the enemy knew they had not overpowered the opposing forces.

- **The STANDARD of THE HOLY GHOST** is lifted when the presence of evil is powerful enough for you to be physically sensitive—e.g., becoming nauseated in the presence of witchcraft, homosexuality, hatred, etc. That is the warning signal to start warfare prayer against the presence of evil.

- **The STANDARD of THE HOLY GHOST** is lifted when He gives you a dream or a vision concerning some evil that Satan is planning against you.

EXAMPLE

I dreamed of a person who had died three years prior; he was coming into my front door, smiling. I said, *"You are not supposed to be here; you are dead."* The person responded with, *"But I am here."* Immediately following this person coming in the door was an unsaved relative under severe and persistent demonic attacks. Knowing that this was a warning from God, I woke up praying and rebuking death. I called this relative, and he confirmed that that same night Satan had almost convinced him to take his life.

- **The STANDARD of THE HOLY GHOST** is lifted when God places a burden for a particular person during a crisis in that person's life.

EXAMPLE

I felt a burden to pray for a dear friend, who is a pastor hundreds of miles away and who is mightily used of God. I called him; he was under so much demonic attack, personal and spiritual, that he really felt like giving up the ministry. We prayed together by phone and bound and rebuked the demons causing the attacks. During this same period, my daughter-in-law, Evangelist Cynthia Butler, living hundreds of miles away (Nebraska) in another direction, called me to ask me about this pastor, stating, *"Something is wrong, I've been praying for him."* I told her to call him and pray with him. The problems did not go away immediately, but the spiritual attack on his ministry was stopped, and HE TOOK THE TERRITORY BACK.

PRAISE AND WORSHIP AS WEAPONS OF WARFARE

Praise is verbally expressing admiration and appreciation for another. If praise is sincere, your mind, attention, and focus should be on the One you are praising and not on yourself. This eliminates Satan from your thoughts. Of course, everyone can praise the Lord (Psalm 150), and He is indeed worthy. However, when the saints praise the Lord, God immediately fellowships with the believers (Psalm 22:3). Fellowship with the Lord brings spiritual joy and, subsequently, strength (Neh. 8:10): strength to fight the enemy, strength to continue the labor, strength to endure the trials.

Praise is faith and builds faith because it is based on the joyful acceptance of the present as part of God's Will for one's present growth and future blessings.

"Giving thanks always for ALL THINGS unto God and the Father in the Name of Our Lord, Jesus Christ." (Eph. 5:20)

Praising God for ALL THINGS includes praising HIM IN ADVERSITY; when the rent is not paid and there is no income, when sickness comes, when children are in total rebellion. Offering the *"sacrifice of praise"* (Hebrews 13:15) suggests that praise is appropriate even when your situation is so difficult, it seems hard to do anything (except praise God). Consider King Jehoshaphat and the children of Israel when they were surrounded and outnumbered by the Ammonites, Edomites, and Moabites. After fasting and praying, the Lord spoke to him:

"And when he had consulted with the people, he appointed singers unto the Lord, and that should praise the beauty of Holiness, as they went out before the army to say PRAISE THE LORD, for his mercy endureth forever. And when they began to sing and to praise, the Lord set ambushments against the children of Ammon, Moab, and Mount Seir which were come against Judah; and they were smitten." (II Chron. 20:21, 22)

Many things happen in the unseen spiritual realm when God's people praise Him. God has hosts of angels, which He will use to minister in human situations (Heb. 1:14; II

Kings 6:15-17). The text suggests that either the Lord magnified the praises of the Israelites so that the attackers believed themselves to be outnumbered and they mistakenly ambushed each other, or the Lord of Hosts[52] could have dispatched warring angels to ambush the children of Ammon, Moab, and Mount Seir.

EXAMPLE

On one occasion during our street services, several men were chasing a lone man. They had huge sticks and bats. Their rage was obvious; it had something to do with a bad drug deal. This man, fleeing for his life, ran in the midst of the saints; we, of course, were unarmed. One of the evangelists, Fay Anderson, a great street evangelist, now deceased, who was ministering the Word of God, immediately began singing one of the powerful praises of the church, *"There is POWER, POWER, WONDER-WORKING POWER IN THE BLOOD."* Each time the men attempted to come among the saints and attack the man, they could not. We could not see anything, but it was very obvious that God had dispatched some angels as we praised God in song to prevent violence to the man or us. We prayed for the man, but he left in a hurry when several men, who apparently were his reinforcements, arrived.

Praise in its truest sense becomes **WORSHIP** when God's people praise Him for who He is, not for what He has done.

---

52   The term "hosts" in the title "Lord of Hosts" refers to the military angels.

Whenever we include ourselves in our praises, it is thanksgiving. **Worship** is only for God, directed toward God and about God. **Worship** acclaims, praises, and glorifies His awesome HOLINESS, EXCELLENCE, MIGHT, LOVE, AND KINDNESS. To the measure of our comprehension, we glorify God because:

GOD IS OMNIPOTENT. *"And I heard as it were the voice of a great multitude, and as the voice of many waters, and as the voice of mighty thunderings, saying, Alleluia: for the Lord God omnipotent reigneth"* (Rev. 19:6).

GOD IS INFINITE. *"Can any hide himself in the secret places that I shall not see him: saith the Lord. Do not I fill the heaven and earth? Saith the Lord"* (Jer. 23:24).

GOD IS SELF-EXISTENT. *"And God said unto Moses, I AM THAT I AM: and he said, Thus shalt thou say unto the children of Israel, I AM hath sent me unto you"* (Ex. 3:14).

GOD IS IMMUTABLE. *Remember the former things of old: for I am God, and there is none else; I am God, and there is NONE ELSE"* (Is. 46:9-11).

GOD IS INCOMPREHENSIBLE. *"O the depth of the riches both of the wisdom and knowledge of God! How unsearchable are his judgments, and his ways past finding out!"* (Romans 11:33).

GOD IS TRUE. *"...According to the faith of God's elect, and the acknowledging of the truth which is after godliness; in hope of eternal life, which God, THAT CANNOT*

LIE, promised before the world began" (Titus 1:1, 2).

GOD IS GRACIOUS. *"But the GOD OF ALL GRACE, who hath called us unto his eternal glory by Christ Jesus, after that ye have suffered a while, make you perfect, stablish, strengthen, settle you"* (I Peter 5:10).

GOD IS STEADFAST. *"My covenant I will not break, nor alter the things that is gone out of my lips"* (Psalm 89:34).

Know that PRAISE AND WORSHIP are powerful instruments of spiritual warfare. As soon as you truly give over to God in adoration and praise, He is present in the midst. God does not, in fact, and cannot leave all of His powerful and marvelous attributes in heaven; they are where His praises are. Therefore, Satan can't stand the saints praising and worshipping God because:

1. By glorifying God, the saints are denying any rule to their **sin nature,** and Satan, therefore, has nothing to work with. Even the scripture indicates that clothing yourself with praise defeats the enemy (Isa. 61:3).

2. The presence of darkness (evil) in the midst of God's people must depart as God receives and accepts the praises of His people. Praise brings Divine Light.

3. Because God abides and/or dwells in the PRAISES of HIS people, faith and assurance are present. In other words, fear flees in the presence of praise (Psalm 22:3).

4. Satan is given a "headache" when God's praises go up; he has to flee because God's presence comes down.

Part of any extended deliverance session should include songs of power and praise ("There Is Power in the Blood," "O, the Blood of Jesus," etc.).

Praying or Speaking in an UNKNOWN TONGUE as a WEAPON OF WAR

Unknown tongues[53] are heavenly languages given by the Holy Spirit as a sign to the unbeliever (I Cor. 14:22) and as a sign to the believer (Mark 16:17). Speaking and/or praying in a heavenly language (not something a person is taught or that was memorized) is an individualized weapon against Satan. There are times in a Christian's walk with the Lord when the spiritual warfare is so extreme that praying normally is inadequate. In these times, the Holy Spirit may make intercession through you and for you in a heavenly language spoken by you (Romans 8:26, 27; Isa 28:11, 12). **Satan does not have the gift of interpretation**; he therefore does not know the content of your prayers. Furthermore, the believer is:

1. In perfect communion and communication with God;

2. Edified and refreshed (I Cor. 14:4).

---

53 The Gift of Tongues and the Gift of Interpretation of Tongues are two entirely different subjects. Read carefully I Corinthians, chapters 12 and 14.

There may often be occasions when you pray or intercede for a person in a regular service and God will have you praying in an unknown tongue. (God is always mindful of personal and private issues that a person is unable to deal with.)

All of our **weapons** (which are not carnal) must be used or Satan will take advantage. It's not enough to understand a weapon, be familiar with it, or even practice with it from time to time. To gain proficiency and success in this ongoing war against Satan, the Christian must never slack in the use of the **TOOLS OF SPIRITUAL WARFARE.**

THE MANDATED DRESS CODE

"Put on the WHOLE ARMOUR OF GOD, that ye may be able to stand against the WILES of the devil… Wherefore TAKE UNTO YOU THE WHOLE ARMOUR OF GOD that ye may be able to withstand in the evil day, and having done all, TO STAND.

"STAND THEREFORE, having your loins girt about WITH TRUTH, and having on the BREASTPLATE of RIGHTEOUSNESS; And your feet SHOD with the preparation of the GOSPEL OF PEACE; Above all, taking THE SHIELD OF FAITH wherewith ye shall be able to quench ALL THE FIERY DARTS OF THE WICKED. And take the HELMET OF SALVATION and THE SWORD OF THE SPIRIT, which is the WORD OF GOD."
(Eph. 6:11, 13-17)

The dress code of all Christians is mandated by God. Notice the words *put on, take, taking,* and *having*; these suggest that your will is the deciding factor in dressing with the armor. Moreover, the hidden meaning of *take* and *taking* further suggests wearing **the ARMOR** is perpetual and continuous. In other words, **SPIRITUAL ARMOR** must be worn until each Christian finishes his/her course.

Paul uses the metaphor **"The Whole Armor of God"** because of the observations he made watching the Roman soldiers while he was imprisoned. The armor was worn to protect every vulnerable area of the soldier's body. However, this armor covered mainly the front of the soldier because retreating was never an option. In fact, the ancient Roman armies were trained to win; they would be killed by their own leaders if they lost. The interesting parallel is that without constant spiritual preparedness (wearing, maintaining, and using the spiritual armor), **the battle will be lost and spiritual death inevitable.**

1. The Loin Belt of Truth

The loin belt, mentioned first in the text, supported several pieces of the soldier's armor; the breastplate was fastened to the loin belt, the sword (and the lance) was hung on the loin belt, and the shield could also be attached to the loin belt. The loin belt was so important to the soldier, he could not fight and survive without it; he could not wear his armor without it. The believer's loin belt of TRUTH IS JESUS, who said "I am the Way, the Truth and the Light" (John 14:26).

Every Christian's walk with the Lord is based on the **Word**

of God. Understanding, accepting, and living by the Word of God **(THE TRUTH)** determines **ALL** of your Christian experience. After reading and studying the Word, it must come ALIVE in you. This will only happen when you prayerfully meditate on the Word. Find those scriptures that relate to your concerns and use them, even in your prayer life.

2. The Breastplate of Righteousness

The breastplate was beautiful and shining, made either of brass or bronze. It would shine magnificently in sunlight and would reflect light. Righteousness is that character or quality of being just, honest, fair, moral, and right.

Further, **righteousness** is protection from slander, malignity, and character assassination. When you have walked so circumspectly that you have always abstained from ALL appearance of evil (I Thess. 5:23), Satan cannot defile your reputation and thus kill your influence. **Righteousness** is not a struggle because we are the *"righteousness of God in Christ Jesus"* (II Cor. 5:21). In other words, living righteously like the Apostle Paul wrote is by faith: ***"...the life which I now live in the flesh I live by the faith of the Son of God..."*** **(Gal. 2:20).**

Notice that sanctification (quitting, laying aside, and putting off all that you know is wrong) is part of your **righteousness**; sanctification is taught from the Word of God. **Righteousness** is also a protective safety net because of divine retribution: ***"Be not deceived, God is not mocked: for whatsoever a man soweth, that shall he also reap"*** **(Gal. 6:7).** ***"Sow to yourselves in righteousness, reap in mercy..."***

(Hosea 10:12).

"The sinners in Zion are afraid; trembling has seized the godless: 'Who among us can live with the devouring fire? Who among us can live with everlasting flames?' HE THAT WALKETH RIGHTEOUSLY, and speaketh uprightly..." (Isa. 33:15)

3. Feet SHOD with the Preparation of the GOSPEL OF PEACE

The Roman soldiers' shoes were very sophisticated and strong. The shoes were made with two pieces of metal, top and bottom; the sides were held together with several pieces of leather. At times in combat, spikes, which were over two inches long, were attached to the bottom of the shoes. The word *shod* is derived from the word *hupodeomai,* which suggests the idea of "binding something tightly."

Peace is bound in the hearts and minds because of PEACE WITH GOD (salvation): *"And through him God was pleased to reconcile to himself all things, whether on earth or in heaven, BY MAKING PEACE THROUGH THE BLOOD OF HIS CROSS. And you who were once estranged..., he has now reconciled..."* (Col. 1:20, 21). Because we have PEACE WITH GOD, we dare not dishonor His love, His sacrifice, His mercy, by not being purveyors of peace. Since God HATES those who *"sow discord among the brethren"* (Prov. 6:19), it is mandatory (because we are wearing all of the armor) *"...to let the peace of God rule..."* (Col. 3:15).

Your feet shod with the **GOSPEL OF PEACE** strongly suggests that in any situation of conflict and strife, the believer must be God's mediator (with prayer, counseling, arbitration, or whatever it takes). Proclaiming the **GOSPEL OF PEACE** is part of the Christian's ability to overcome.

4. The Shield of Faith

The SHIELD of the Roman soldier protected the entire front of his body; it was always in the soldier's hand or attached to his LOIN BELT. It was made of six layers of thick animal hide woven together so tightly, it was like a strong metal, a protective device like today's bulletproof vest. The Roman soldier had to care for his shield every day by rubbing oil on it to keep the shield from becoming hard and brittle. Furthermore, the enemy in those days made darts that burned even as they went into human flesh. A normal injury from a dart was bad enough, but a deep puncture wound full of fire meant sudden death. The shield, covering most of the body, was effective in preventing these fiery darts from finding their mark. First, all who are saved are given a measure of faith (Romans 12:3); faith to be saved, maybe faith to minister, etc. How is faith generated and increased? By and with **THE WORD OF GOD.**

> *"Faith cometh by hearing and hearing by the Word of God."* **(Romans 10:17)**

Biblically we define faith as *"…the substance of things HOPED for, the evidence of things not seen"* **(IIebrews 11:1).** Hope is not a longing or desire, but "confident expectation—assurance." The Word of God, alive in the believer, allows the believer to set his/her face as flint, not wavering or slacking because of the promises in THE WORD OF GOD. The promises of the Word of God include His power (Luke 10:19); His protection (Isaiah 54:17); and His victory (I John 5:4). The believer can block all "fiery darts" of discouragement, fear, loneliness, rage, etc. because of the promises in the Word of God.

5. The Helmet of Salvation

The Roman soldier's helmet was beautiful, decorative, and impressive-looking. It could be recognized for miles. Further, it covered the head COMPLETELY, even covering a good portion of the neck. Because it was made of brass or bronze, two of the strongest metals of that day, it could not be pierced by any metal of the time.

The mind is the bridge for the body and man's spirit. The mind is also the door to man's body and spirit.[54] *"For to be carnally minded is death..."* (Romans 8:6) means a failure to align the thoughts with the Will of Christ, which prefaces spiritual death (a backslidden condition).[55] Take for example how often in life everyone gets hurt, offended, mistreated, abused, criticized, and/or ignored. It is natural to want to defend oneself or get revenge. Jesus said to forgive seventy times seven in a day, if necessary (Matt. 18:22). Notice, He asked His Father to forgive those who WERE PUTTING HIM TO DEATH (Luke 23:34).

54　For a more detailed discussion on how Satan seeks to control the mind, read the chapter called "The Mind Game" in *Called to Be Saints,* by Fay Ellis Butler.

55　Phil 4:8.

"For though we walk in the flesh, we do not war after the flesh. (For the weapons of our warfare are not carnal, but mighty through God to the pulling down of strong holds;) Casting down imaginations and every high thing that exalteth itself against the knowledge of God, and bringing into captivity every thought to the obedience of Christ." **(II Cor. 10: 3-5)**

At any and all cost, the believer must have *"the mind of Christ"* (Phil. 2:5). The Mind of Christ was one of total humility and absolute obedience to the Will of His Father. He gave up His deity and put on humanity to live in the midst of sin, to be abused by sinners and then to become SIN FOR US, all to please His Father. Also just as Christ shed His heavenly divinity to do the Will of God at a great cost, the saint, too, must be willing to pay any price that it takes to please God. When that kind of decision is made for God, then your salvation is protected, and there is no wavering. *"A DOUBLE MINDED man is unstable in all his ways"* (James 1:8).

The **"helmet"** fits and remains securely in place when we abide in the Words of Jesus: *"...If any man will come after me, let him deny himself, and take up his cross and follow me"* (Matt. 11:29). The *mind of Christ,* that is, being obedient even in times of suffering, is not an automatic mind-set; it is cultivated daily, with the Word of God — the Bible — and in prayer. Like the Roman soldier had to put his helmet on and wear it continuously in battle to be protected, similarly believers must daily look to Jesus in order to be like Jesus.

The **helmet of salvation** is the protection that comes from absolute, at-any-cost obedience to Christ and humility. The helmet of obedience and humility keeps your transformed mind RENEWED (Romans 12:2) and SOUND (II Tim. 1:7). You are confident that Satan will be defeated in your presence.

6. The Sword of the Spirit, Which is the Word of God

The Roman warriors used several different swords in combat. The Greek word *machira* is the word for the sword used in this text. This particular sword was a vicious murder weapon, a foot and a half long, and razor sharp on both sides; the end of the sword was curved slightly. Usually the sword was used to pierce the abdomen and twist while in the abdomen; the curved end would pull intestines out when this sword was removed. In those days, emergency medical teams did not exist, nor trauma teams in hospitals. When this sword was used, death was certain. It would be the same as a 45 magnum bullet piercing and exploding in your abdomen. All the emergency and trauma equipment in this country today would be hopeless.

The Word of God is sharper than any two-edged *machira (*sword). *Rhema* is Greek for *Word* in this text. *Rhema* has a meaning somewhat different from *Logos* (which is another Greek word for *word*). *Rhema* specifically refers to the Holy Spirit working life-changing power with **the Word of God.** When the **Word of God** comes in Anointing and Power, the person who is not in a relationship with God (the spirit man is dead) BECOMES FULLY AWARE HOW FAR HE/SHE IS FROM GOD. Therefore, *the Rhema of God,* dividing asunder soul and spirit, penetrates, convicts, and changes carnal minds to made-up minds for a surrendered life; in other words, a decision is made to allow the Spirit of God to sanctify and live in the human spirit.

The Roman sword was one of power, authority, and judgment wielded by the trained soldier. Likewise the Christian in full battle gear has life-changing authority using the Anointed Word of God. **The Sword of the Spirit,** the Anointed Offensive Weapon, must be cultivated and worked on faithfully and consistently by every believer.

The Roman soldier's armor had to fit him properly if he was going to be effective and successful in battle. Each Christian must recognize that **the Armor**, which is mandated for all, must be maintained according to each person's specific needs. For example, the child raised in Sunday School and protected from the filth of the world (drugs, promiscuous sex, demonic music) must wear **armor,** but because of the foundations of clean moral living, the maintenance of the armor will not be the same as one whose lifestyle was opposite. The **helmet of salvation** (the "do-right mind") may be easier to maintain if the individual does not have to struggle with excessive temptation from the past.

The Armor is a graphic metaphor for spiritual preparedness against unseen evil and will also protect, not only against human enemies (with wicked plans) but also against the individual **sin nature.** You will notice an overview of **all of the Armor** deals with the mind being disciplined in the Word of God. Satan, full of wisdom, has thousands of ways to corrupt and defeat anyone. The only defense and offense against Satan is to get in the Word; memorize it, study it, and meditate upon it.[56] Then, ALWAYS remain prepared for war.

To be a skilled warrior, always ready for any battle, requires dedication—always keepings one's warrior skills honed. It is not always easy to go on consecrations—days of fasting and prayer only. It is not always convenient to study and meditate on the Word. It is quite often difficult to spend time in prayer every day, particularly if you are working and have a family to attend to. However, Satan is working 24/7 to take you and your family to hell with him. So spiritual tasks for constant preparedness are not an option; they are a must. Remember, people may not know when you have failed to maintain your warrior status, but God and the devil certainly know.

Being a WARRIOR is not an option. It is a MANDATE from God!

"Behold I give unto you POWER to tread on serpents and scorpions and over ALL the power of the enemy, and nothing shall by any means hurt you." **(Luke 10:19)**

---

56 See Appendix III for a Bible memorization plan.

TACTICS AND STRATEGY

Tactics, a military term, has to do with expedient plans for achieving a specific goal. Strategy, likewise a military term, relates to the science or art of overall planning and conduct for large-scale, long-term military battles. The **WAR IS ON** and since Satan is the "prince of this world," **THE WAR ZONE IS EVERYWHERE**, in your children's school, on the job, in the church, in the street, in the playground, in the choir, etc.

Satan and all the powers of darkness were defeated at Calvary and the Resurrection (Col. 2:15). Victory is certain only if the church keeps Satan and his demons defeated. This doesn't happen just because the believer prays, *"Yes, Lord"* or because the believer fasts and prays. This happens because every child of God recognizes Satan's strategies and **ACTIVELY** fights the enemy with all **the weapons** that God has given. The fight is not haphazard; it is planned and targeted.

HOW TO RECOGNIZE DEMONIC ATTACKS:

Against yourself

First, observe your feelings, your sleep patterns, and your thoughts. If you do not like what you are feeling, dreaming, and thinking, it is not you. No one goes around giving themselves bad feelings, dreams, or thoughts, **BUT SATAN DOES** inject these into the mind. Jesus promised, *"Peace I leave with you, my peace I give unto you: not as the world giveth, give I unto you. Let not your heart be troubled, neither let it be afraid"* (John 14:27). When you are restless, anxious about everything, tormented, it is not you; it is Satan. Following restlessness and anxiety are usually **spirits of affliction** (asthma, hypertension, or heart disease, etc.) because the body needs rest. Never ask "Why am I going through this?" Once you ask why, you are claiming, accepting, and agreeing with Satan's attack. Just keep rebuking him.

When you feel as though you weigh 1,000 pounds in the morning, that is an immobilizing **spirit of depression.** Depression will remain for years if it is not recognized as a demon and dealt with as such (See Isaiah 61:3). Never ask why. Rebuke depression and keep your mind on God with praise until depression leaves.

In addition, believers accept oppression from the enemy because they believe they are being punished for past mistakes. One must differentiate between reaping visible results for past deeds and the demons that precipitated the past deeds.

For example, an out-of-wedlock child is here to stay, but the lust that caused it can be dispossessed. Satan will of course try and return with the old feelings and behavior, but Jesus has given every believer POWER over **all the power of the enemy** (Luke 10:19). ALL OPPRESSION is of the devil; deal with it as you would any demon.

Against your home

Always be conscious of the social interaction in your home. If the children are always bickering and arguing, **your family is under satanic attack.** If marriage partners find themselves becoming unreasonably angry at one another or unreasonably resentful toward the in-laws, **the marriage is under satanic attack.** If you have one financial disaster after another, including burglary and robbery, **you are under attack.** Never just passively accept such things as the "trials of life." FIGHT the devil with the weapons of your warfare.

Against your church

When the choir members are continuously angry and bickering in choir rehearsals, **the church is under attack.** When the clubs and auxiliaries begin competing or will only support their own special projects, **the church is under attack.** When slothfulness sets in and the church doors close Sunday nights and weeknights, **the church is under attack.** When it becomes expeditious to stand up praying at the beginning of the service for five minutes, instead of praying on your knees for an hour, **the church is under serious satanic attack.** When the pastor sounds angry in his messages, or becomes sick just once too often, or begins having trouble with his family, **THE CHURCH IS UNDER ATTACK.** When the members stop tithing, the church is under attack. (If individuals are cursed with a curse for not tithing and they attend your church, their curses follow them to church. God helps the church in which the majority of the members do not tithe.) While we must always offer God our praises, a church under attack needs serious fasting and warfare prayers.

HOW TO BIND AND CAST THE DEVIL OUT:

First of all, **be certain that you are really in the Body of Christ,** because Satan has power. The only power that stops and defeats him is the Power of God. Never make the mistake of the seven sons of Sceva (Acts 19:14). These sons attempted to cast the devil out of ONE MAN. The demons in this man overpowered them and left them wounded and naked, because these seven sons were not saved. In fact, the demons said, *"Paul I know and Jesus I know, but who are you."* Remember, Satan will only honor the Blood of Jesus applied to your life. He does not honor looks, money, gifts, ability, or connections, only the Power of God through His Son, Jesus. It can be dangerous for any individual to "lay hands" without the assurance of the Holy Ghost because Satan may erupt in the presence of powerlessness.

Secondly, **be sure to bind any demon first;** if not bound, it will try to enter someone else. ***Truly I tell you, whatever you bind on earth will be bound in heaven, and whatever you loose on earth will be loosed in heaven (Matt 18:18).***
Often you hear of people binding demons and sending them to "the lake." That is incorrect. They are not going to the

lake yet. **Bind the demons IN THE NAME OF JESUS,** because you are standing in His stead as a joint heir with Him (Romans 8:17). If you want to send them someplace, send them to "dry places" according to Matthew 12:44.

Third, **cast the demons out IN THE NAME OF JESUS.**

If you are not sure that it is a demon acting up in a person, **plead the Blood of Jesus.** Remember, Jesus cannot hurt Himself, nor does He work against Himself. Therefore, if it is not a demon, **pleading the Blood of Jesus will not do any harm.**

In these days, the churches are experiencing Satan actually sending his workers to the church. They will act like and dress like the people of God. Their job is to disrupt the godly functions and kingdom work of the church. Ask God **to open your spiritual eyes** as he did Elisha's servant (II Kings 6:17), and keep them open. When these persons come into your church services and you recognize the evil in them, begin BINDING THE DEVIL IMMEDIATELY IN THE NAME OF JESUS. Usually these persons do not want to be free—you can't, and God will not override their wills—but they can be BOUND by believers IN THE NAME OF JESUS.

EXAMPLE

On one Sunday morning, just before service began, a young man came in the church and stated, "I'm going to kill everybody." He was quiet, looked intense, but determined. We quietly prayed and bound the devil's plans without fear. That young man stood in the back with his arms up in a karate position of attack for at least an hour or more. As the service continued, we never stopped quietly BINDING THE DEVIL and rendering his plans **ineffective through the shed Blood of Jesus.** The young man finally departed halfway during the service.

There will be some who do not want to be free. However, in spite of that form of rebellion, the believer can still bind the devil in that person to stop evil.

Something is desperately and seriously wrong if the church cannot bind any demon that seeks to take over the services. To my horror, one pastor informed me that he HAD MOVED THE LOCATION OF HIS CHURCH because the drug addicts and drunks repeatedly came in and disrupted services. Further, Mark 16:16-18 suggests that if you are unable to bind and cast out demons IN THE NAME OF JESUS, you are NOT a believer. Do your first works all over again and put on the whole armor of God and KEEP IT ON.

HOW TO RESIST THE DEVIL:

"Be sober, be vigilant; because your adversary the devil, as a roaring lion, walketh about, seeking whom he may devour: whom resist steadfast in the faith..." **(I Peter 5:8, 9)**

"Submit yourselves therefore to God. Resist the devil, and he will flee from you." **(James 4:7)**

"To resist" means to **strive or work against; fight off; oppose actively**; also **to remain firm against the action or effect of; withstand.** Notice that lions or any predator will attack and devour victims who are not alert and/or who are young, weak, or sick. Satan will send enough trials, temptations, and/or tribulations to weaken and get the believer centering on him/herself usually with self-pity, rejection, maybe even hopelessness.

Resist personal onslaughts of Satan by:

1. Seeking a spiritual confidant and talking together and praying one for another (James 5:16).

2. *Neither give place to the devil* by refusing to accept the thoughts he attempts to inject in your mind. (You refuse by disciplining your mind to think on positive things (Phil. 4:8) or by quoting scripture out loud as often as those negative thoughts come.)

3. By identifying those weaknesses and dealing with them in the light of the Word. For example, if you were sexually active and unmarried prior to accepting the Lord, you cannot, you must not, watch most of what comes on TV because it is lust, lust, and more lust. *"...Let us lay aside every weight and sin that doth so easily beset us..."* **(Romans 12:1).**

4. By learning and using the Word to fight satanic attacks on the mind. A believer must **never, never, never** question why he/she is feeling a certain way or why thoughts of the past are tormenting the mind. As

soon as the believer begins to question why he/she has claimed ownership to the thoughts and feelings, she or he has placed him/herself in Satan's territory. Any and every thought or feeling that you dislike and you don't want, fight it with the Blood of Jesus, the Name of Jesus, and the Word of God. Learn, for your own survival, I John 4:4; Luke 10:19; Numbers 10:35; 23:19.

Resist the attacks by the devil in your local church:

1. Always pray for the pastor and the ministry of the church.

2. Never be part of spreading any kind of truth or untruth that is not beneficial to the body (Prov. 6:18, 19).

3. Be very specific when in prayer in the church. Yes, pray, HAVE YOUR WAY, LORD! But also **take authority over** counterfeit spirits, religious demons, spirits of deception, and delusion; BIND and REBUKE them in THE NAME OF JESUS OF NAZARETH. Rest assured that in every church, there will be individuals going ahead of God, doing and saying what God has not given them to do or say.

4. For any person ministering that you know is not of God, remember what the Word of God promised: *"Again I say unto you, that if two of you shall agree on earth as touching anything that they shall ask, it shall be done for them of my Father which is in*

Heaven" (**Matt. 18:19**). This is a confirmed promise that any two believers with the Holy Spirit praying against any evil in the church shall defeat the evil.

EXAMPLE

At one church in my community, the pastor and founder died; his wife became the pastor. She was in her eighties and tired. Satan sent one loud, aggressive, so-called evangelist to this church. The pastor needing help allowed this person to chair the services. This woman's religious demons had her loudly jumping all over, praying for everyone, and dominating the service and the atmosphere. Strangely, the times I was invited, even in a two-week revival, this woman did not come to the services. God gave me to explain Matthew 18:19 to the faithful members and instruct them on how to be spiritually tough and agree in prayer every time this woman attempted to manipulate the service. The first Sunday three members started PLEADING THE BLOOD of Jesus as soon as the so-called evangelist began; that Sunday she could not get started. After two more Sundays of the faithful prayer warriors "touching and agreeing" in spiritual warfare, this woman left and has never returned.

HOW TO DEAL WITH A DEMON-POSSESSED PERSON:

Demon possession is real and a powerfully dangerous condition. When Satan has walked into and/or in and out of a person's body, soul, and spirit, that person is demon possessed. The person can bark like an actual dog, wiggle like a snake, go into a trance, or act as if they are dead. The person actually has no control over speech or actions and may in fact not recall many of his/her activities while possessed.

First of all, you must make sure you are saved and filled with the Baptism of the Holy Ghost. Secondly, make sure you have prepared yourself by fasting and praying.

"...His disciples asked him privately, Why could not we cast him out? And he said unto them, This kind come forth by nothing, but by prayer and fasting." (Mark 9:28, 29)[57]

Thirdly, never go alone! There should always be a minimum of two persons when warring against demon possession (See Luke 10:1; Eccl. 4:9). Warring against numerous demons in a person can drain any person physically and spiritually.

If possible, avoid working with the person in their own home. Do not try and work with them in your home. Take them to a neutral place, like the church. Of course, the church may not be available or you may have to begin "fighting" the enemy immediately. God knows the situation. The first thing you must always do is pray for yourself and your partner and "cover yourselves with THE BLOOD OF JESUS."

Everything you do should be Bible-based. If Satan is

---

57 Today the warfare is so serious, that each Christian needs to be filled with the Holy Spirit, praying and fasting all the time. Satan is so bold, any day now, he is going to challenge you and your church. BE READY!

dominating the person to the point where the person cannot speak with their voice (the demons are using their vocal cords), you bind and cast out as many demons as you can recognize. If you cannot identify any demons, you can be sure that there are foul demons, unclean demons, mind-controlling demons, demons of rejection, etc.: cast them out. There will be a point when the person will be able to use their own voice. As soon as this is possible, insist that he/she REPENTS TO GOD over and over again. Have them ask Jesus into their lives.

Repentance makes deliverance easier. Repentance serves notice on Satan that he has no legal right to oppress or possess this person any longer. Once the person has repented, he/she can also start "pleading the Blood of Jesus" against the devil.

> *"And they OVERCAME him by the BLOOD OF THE LAMB, and by the Word of their testimony; and the loved not their lives unto death."* (Rev. 12:11)

All the while you are ministering to that person, the demons will be talking to their mind. The demons, liars all of them, will tell the person they are going to kill them; sometimes those demons will choke them and they will turn blue. This is to frighten the "warriors" and the demon-possessed person. Just bind these manifestations and rebuke all lying demons. Furthermore, Satan and all of his demons love to be seen and heard; they are delighted to be given an opportunity to brag. Be certain that after a while, some of them will boldly tell you without being asked, "I am Lucifer (or Baal or Isis) and

I am not coming out." If you are unsure of the demons you are confronting, remember that God wants this person out of the possession of Satan (II Peter. 3:9). Therefore, ask the Lord for the discerning you need for this deliverance session (I John 5:14, 15). It is always better to ask the Lord what you are dealing with, because if you ask the demon-possessed person, the demons will lie. In fact, stronger demons in a person will force weaker demons out to fool the warriors. The test is always to ask the person to say **"Jesus, is my Resurrected Lord."** Demons will never say this.

If it is a long deliverance session, don't wear yourself out! Keep the pressure on the enemy but sing some deliverance songs like "There is power, wonder-working Power in the Blood" or "What can wash away my sin," etc.

You will find that when the person begins acting worse, those demons are being "unshackled," and they will soon come out. When the person is freed or delivered, he/she will automatically start praising God. As this person continues to do this, if there is any residue, God will deliver from that also because God will enter His own praises (Psalm 22:3). Where God enters, Satan must retreat.

Always ask the person before ending, "Is there anything else we need to deal with?" Usually, these persons will be glad to confess anything else that is hidden. Never leave the person without instructing them what to expect, how they should fast and pray and read the Word of God.[58]

---

58   The book *After Deliverance, Then What?* by Fay Ellis Butler was written specifically for persons who have been or will be manipulated, oppressed, or possessed by Satan after their deliverance.

HOW TO "CLEAN" AND "SEAL" YOUR HOME:

All too often the believers fail to fully understand "deception," which is "misrepresentation," "falsehood," "seduction," and "being beguiled." Most Christians believe their homes are safe havens. If you have unsaved children or an unsaved spouse, your house is not "clean" of evil spirits. If you have children of any age who are unsupervised after school, your home is not clean of evil.

- **Television**: Too much of what you see as entertainment on television is lust, violence, and witchcraft. You can recognize Satan in so much of what comes on television. You also watch church services on TV and they certainly minister the presence of God right where you are in your own home. Realize that Satan is doing the same thing, testifying lust, rape, murder, and witchcraft to your home and LEAVING A PRESENCE there. How often have you awakened very tired after fighting in your sleep? THE TELEVISION WAS LEFT ON and violence was testifying to your spirit while you were asleep. Have you had infants and young children in your family having nightmares for no reason that you can discern? Have you considered the horror movies watched in your home may be the reason? If your home is going to be cleaned of evil, TURN OFF THE FILTH. You would not feed yourself rancid rat meat or macerated maggots; don't pollute your home and mind with a visual diet of filth. Obviously, if you live with unsaved persons, this is difficult. Remember, we are at war.

Offset any pollution from unsaved relatives' choices of entertainment by PLAYING BIBLE TAPES AS OFTEN AS POSSIBLE (very softly if necessary); it will still be effective.

- **Music:** Much of the rap music, rock, hip hop and other music seems to be inspired by Satan, with sexually suggestive lyrics. This music is played everywhere: in the stores, in the streets, in cars, on the radio, on the television, with video and tapes, etc. Many of the chords are like incantations that invite demons into your home while the music is playing; the beat is often as hypnotic as voodoo drums. You cannot prevent your unsaved relatives from doing certain things while you are not present. But you can keep an aggressive war going on against Satan's invasive tactics in your home. Always play your Bible tapes. Satan hates Revelations, particularly chapter 20. Regularly pray aloud in your home and declare that the atmosphere belongs to God.

- **Books and Literature:** Satan has inspired many to write satanic-demon-magnifying books, whether they are novels or other genres. These books affect the minds of those who read them, but in addition, because it is satanic material, demons will be attached to those books.

EXAMPLE

A friend recently purchased a new home and asked me to come and pray in her home. I specifically enquired of her if the former owners had left anything. She told me that the former owner was a Mason, and he had left his Mason's Bible, which he planned to come for. If he took everything he wanted, he should have taken this Bible. I told her to get the Mason's Bible out of her house. We anointed each room and prayed throughout the house. For the next two months, she began suddenly having a series of medical problems, including a thyroid condition, a breast problem, a heart problem, etc., which she did not have before. (She is a nurse and a single, hardworking parent who raised her two daughters alone. She was never a hypochondriac.) She was even admitted into the hospital for a period of time. She called me very agitated about all these problems. I asked her, "Is that Bible still in your home?" Her reply was, *"I forgot to take it out."* As soon as she removed that Bible from her house and prayed again, all of the medical problems subsided.

- **Art :** In many societies artisans and craftsmen are initiates in secret societies. Many of their art works and artifacts are sold in this country. Take for instance the Kachini dolls, which are the dolls of the medicine men of some of the Native Americans in the west.

EXAMPLE

I was ministering to a young woman in New Mexico who admitted to having purchased some artwork that was used in some of the Plains Indians' rituals. She admitted that the Lord told her to get rid of it. She loved the piece and thought if she prayed in her home, it would be all right. IT WAS NOT ALL RIGHT. Her daughters, in their teens, having been raised in the church, began acting out right after she purchased this artifact—promiscuity, partying, hanging out late, etc. The Lord showed her that the artifact "gave place to multiple demons" in her home, which made the innate **sin nature** in her children boldly erupt. (Most times children do not need any help with rebellion; it is natural to them.) She finally "cleaned" her house, but her teenage troubles had begun with a bang; she was still praying and trying to bring her teens under subjection.

Each Christian regularly should get the oil, pray in every room in the house, anointing the walls, windows, and doors. Always let Satan know this home belongs to the Lord. Since Satan hates the Word of God, get some Bible tapes and play them often.

EXAMPLE

When I was writing the book *Called to Be Saints*, Satan was constantly sending interference. I would forget to regularly save the material on the computer; something would happen, like a book falling on the plug and disconnecting the electricity. Valuable information that the Lord had just helped me to write would be lost. My hands and feet would burn and itch (I never have had a problem with nerves). If I scratched them or put them in cold water, it worsened. I even had episodes of diarrhea from a nervous stomach. I realized that I was under demonic attack because Satan did not want the book written. Finally it occurred to me that this was a specifically planned, orchestrated attack that I was not fighting properly. I began playing my Bible tapes EVERY DAY in my study. I began thanking God for helping me to write. I refused to focus on the devil and worry.

The Christian can never be sure of the how Satan is coming next, but he is coming. Like the Boy Scout motto, believers must always be prepared. We must be faithful with **our armor,** using the WORD OF GOD skillfully, keeping our homes safe, peaceful, and cleaned of all evil. ALWAYS PRAY IN YOUR HOME.

HOW TO "TRY A SPIRIT":

"Beloved, DO NOT BELIEVE every spirit, but try the spirits, to see whether they are of God; because many false prophets have gone out into the world." **(I John 4:1)**

In these times, many false prophets and false teachers will enter the churches and minister. TRY or TEST all ministers and ministries. There are two areas to be tested: the message and the lives of the teachers, preachers, prophets, or evangelists. If the message seems to be biblically sound and their lives do not measure up, **that is still a problem.**

You must look at the messenger.

a) **Listen for their confession.**

Does his moral character correspond with those mentioned in the Word of God (Isa. 28:7; Jer. 6:13; Jer. 23:14)? There are false prophets with the spirit of the antichrist WHO NEVER KNEW GOD specifically targets weak Christians. These appear as "angels of light" and will work "lying wonders" because too many believers have "itching ears." These persons can be detected as workers of Satan if you **TRY them by the Word of God.** Confessing that Jesus has come in the flesh includes several important things. First, to be able to say JESUS IS LORD is a testimony that "I have accepted the work at Calvary and the Resurrection and now He is in control of my life." When the "false workers" get up to minister, the devil in them will never allow them to say **Jesus is Lord of my life.** Secondly, these false workers will never say anything like "The Resurrection Power rules in me." Thirdly, they will never pray at any time during their message or ministry, "Father, IN THE NAME OF JESUS OF NAZARETH, I BIND, REBUKE, AND CAST OUT all contrary demons, all hindering demons, and every demon that opposes the Work of God in this service."

EXAMPLE

I was participating in a women's retreat where a so-called great prophetess was ministering in the night service. This woman looked strange, acted strange, and was strange. Her skirt was very short, she kicked off her shoes, and for over two hours she bounced around the room to a drumbeat and spoke in a cadence. She said some demonic things like "Let your wills go and receive the spirit." The Bible never speaks of having a passive will; it emphasizes using your will with *let, put on, put off,* etc. She never told the people to agree with God's will and ask Jesus to become Lord of their lives. She never at any time rebuked the devil or any demons in any person. She spoke of receiving thirty-, sixty-, and hundred-fold miracles using the Kingdom parable of the woman with the three portions of leaven (Matt. 13:33). This was a total misrepresentation of scripture. She prophesied glowing things to people, laid hands on them, and they fell with FROWNS on their faces. She was A WITCH sent and "anointed" by Satan and not just someone who got caught up in their flesh. It was difficult to pray against this witch. I realized she had been invited by the church leaders, the people believed in her ministry and/or had "itching ears," and they were opening up to her. All of this strengthened her evil work.

b) **Listen to the message.**

Theological apostasy is rampant. In many churches a simple confession of faith without sanctification will be propagated. People will not be instructed in absolute obedience to God's Word and therefore will not be able to receive the baptism of the Holy Spirit according to Acts 5:32. People are then taught how to **receive** religious demons; *"Listen and speak what you hear"* or *"Just relax your mouth and say whatever comes to you."*

Theological apostasy includes entertainment gospel that

does not convict but makes people feel good enough to shout, sing, dance, and give money. This is also the spirit of the antichrist.

"But there were false prophets also among the people, even just as there shall be false teachers among you who privily shall bring in damnable heresies, even denying the Lord that bought them, and bring upon themselves destruction." **(I Peter. 2:1-3)**

c) **Observe their MO (modus operandi).**

Does the messenger always attempt to please God (I Thess. 2:2, 4)?

Some leaders instruct individuals more concerning following rules and traditions than training them into becoming disciples and teaching them how to hear and obey God. In some places, rules for submitting to leadership and church dogma are so excessive, it is like mind-control (witchcraft without the occult trappings). Church bondage becomes so powerful that meeting obligations and attending services become more important than witnessing, missions, or even "calling a solemn assembly" for prayer and consecration. These shifts in focus are caused by the spirit of the antichrist.

Work at developing greater discernment

First of all, **learn to become sensitive to how the Lord deals with you.** When your spirit becomes troubled in a service while someone is ministering, **ask the Lord about it**. If you find yourself "pleading the Blood of Jesus" (without at first realizing it) when someone is up speaking, **ask the Lord about it.** Do not assume if you are uncomfortable in a service that something is wrong with you.

Then the question of what to do is relevant. If you have listened and "tried the spirit" and it is not of God, **then do not agree with that spirit. Don't open yourself to that spirit!** DO NOT ACCEPT PRAYER FROM THAT PERSON. If that person is leading the congregation in praise in the microphone, don't praise the Lord with that spirit. Pray out loud BUT PRAY SOMETHING DIFFERENT, LIKE *"Lord, bind the devil, cast the devil out in the Name of Jesus. Have Your way."* Never strengthen a demon by praying or praising with him/her.

HOW TO TRAIN AND PROTECT YOUR CHILDREN:

Children are precious to God. Always let them know that they are very precious and God's love is with them all the time. Have them pray the "sinner's prayer" as young as they are able to understand. I heard my daughter-in-law, Cynthia Butler, state in a revival that if children can learn all the commercials on television, the lyrics to rap music, and try and dance like Michael Jackson as young as two years old, then they can be saved. Lead them to the Lord as soon as possible. Monitor your child's choice of television programs. If necessary, lock the television up when you are not home. Parenting is a spiritual calling and responsibility. Parents are supposed to train their children in the Word of God (Deut. 6: 7) and to love God.

Satan would desire to mess your child up with violence, rape, drugs, or incest and/or mess his/her mind up from filth in the environment (including the television and social networking). Consider your child a future spiritual leader used by God to win his/her generation; START TRAINING HIM/HER NOW. Teach them about the Blood of Jesus, telling them that God will certainly protect them when they pray. Teach them how to pray precise but simple prayers. Get them to memorize at least one Bible verse per week, or at least the memory verse from the Sunday School lesson. Every day before sending your child out to play or to school, pray a brief prayer for them and anoint them with oil.

Always remember that the Holy Spirit in every believer is the only reason Satan is still restrained in the earth. Therefore, learn to exercise all of your rights in God:

RESIST the devil IN JESUS' NAME,

**RENOUNCE everything that hinders
your sanctification IN JESUS' NAME,**

BIND the devil IN JESUS' NAME,

REBUKE the devil IN JESUS' NAME,

CAST the devil out IN JESUS' NAME.

Power only becomes power when the resources of power are utilized. Yes, being saved, sanctified, and filled with the Holy Spirit is important. The Holy Spirit is POWER but is only evidenced when the believer prays the Blood of Jesus and uses the Name of Jesus in all prayer.

Being a WARRIOR is not an option.

It is a MANDATE from God!

"Now thanks be unto God, which ALWAYS CAUSES US TO TRIUMPH in Christ, and maketh manifest the savor of his knowledge by us in every place." **(II Cor. 2:14)**

CONCLUSION

Every day the satanic war against the Body of Christ intensifies. That's why you see churches closing, ministries failing, and the churches becoming less powerful. At the same time Satan uses stratagems (cares, burden, worries) to keep individuals sidetracked from hungering and thirsting after righteousness. *"And the cares of this world, and the deceitfulness of riches, and the lusts of other things entering in, **choke the Word**, and it becometh unfruitful"* (Mark 4:19).

Be prayerful and watchful. Wear the **WHOLE ARMOR OF GOD** all the time—**the helmet of salvation, the breastplate of righteousness, the shield of faith, the loin belt of truth, feet shod with the preparation of the Gospel of peace and the sword of the Spirit.** You know God and God knows you, so testify to yourself and Satan every day:

I AM a new creature (II Cor. 5:17) .

I AM a son/daughter of God (John 1:12; Romans 8:14; I John 3:1, 2).

I AM an ambassador for Christ (II Cor. 5:20).

I AM the righteousness of God in Christ Jesus (II Cor. 5.21).

I AM a joint-heir with Christ (Romans 8:17).

I AM an heir of God (Romans 8:17).

I AM protected (Psalm 34:7; 23:3; Isa. 54:17).

I AM prosperous (Joshua 1:8; Psalm 1:2, 3; III John 2).

I AM never alone (Job 5:19-22; Hebrews 13:5).

I AM an overcomer (I John 5:4, 5).

I AM an intercessor (I John 5:14, 15; Jer. 33:3).

I AM full of power (Micah 3:8; Acts 1:8; Luke 10:19).

I AM more than a conqueror (Romans 8:37).

IN ALL CIRCUMSTANCES I MUST KNOW, BELIEVE, AND ACCEPT THE FACT THAT I AM MORE THAN A CONQUEROR. First of all, know that as a believer, you are just a "stranger and pilgrim" here on earth (I Peter 2:11) because Satan has the entire world's political, cultural, religious, economic, and educational systems hostilely organized against God's people. However,

>*"Whatsoever is born of God overcometh the world: and this is the victory that overcometh the World, even our faith."* (I John 5:4)

Faith is the absolute assurance that whatever happens, as a believer, I am yet the winner, because Satan has already been defeated. Notice Paul writes that being more than a conqueror means that you not only defeat the enemy, but you take over his territory. Those who are more than conquerors change every aspect of life. *"Nay, we are more than conquerors through him that loved us"* (Romans 8:37).

For example, Attila the Hun, coming across the steppes of Asia conquering everything in his path as far west into Europe and the Vatican, departed and took his hordes back to Asia. On the other hand, the Spaniards in the 16th century not only conquered a good portion of Latin America, but also destroyed most of the great civilizations; for example, the Incas, the Aztecs, and the Mayas. The Spaniards, who were "more than conquerors," also changed the religions and culture of the region as well as the indigenous languages.[59]

Conquerors must know their enemy and have many tools and plans to control the enemy. Consider that a house can be destroyed gradually from within over a number of years by termites. At the other end of the spectrum, the same house can be leveled in a few seconds by an earthquake or tornado. Many things can destroy a house—fire, floods, tenants, etc. Similarly, the devil, with great wisdom (Ezekiel 28:5), will use many tactics and strategies, gradually or instantly, to destroy your faith and you. Always keep your "warrior mode" strong and consistent. Stay in the Word; use the Word and the Name of Jesus. Remember, the Omnipotent, Omnipresent One is your protector.

---

59   Most of Latin American speak Spanish today except Brazilians.

"I will say of the Lord, He is my refuge and my fortress: MY GOD; in him will I trust. Surely he shall deliver thee from the snare of the fowler, and from the noisome pestilence. He shall cover thee with him feathers, and under his wings shalt thou trust: HIS TRUTH shall be thy shield and buckler. ..Because thou hast made the LORD, which is my refuge, even the most High thou habitation; There shall no evil befall thee, neither shall any plague come nigh thy dwellings." (Psalm 91:2-4, 9.10)

- **MORE THAN A CONQUEROR** means that ALL BELIEVERS can spiritually defeat Satan and then take the territory and seal the territory in victory with THE BLOOD OF JESUS (Rev.12:11).

- **MORE THAN A CONQUEROR** means that ALL BELIEVERS have the right and the responsibility to BIND evil, REBUKE evil, and even SEND demons back to dry places IN THE NAME OF JESUS OF NAZARETH (Matt. 12:43; 18:18).

- **MORE THAN A CONQUEROR** means that ALL BELIEVERS can cover themselves with the BLOOD OF JESUS; cover their possessions with THE BLOOD OF JESUS; and cover their children with THE BLOOD OF JESUS. **Realize that Satan cannot penetrate or violate THE BLOOD OF JESUS** (Rev. 12:11).

- **MORE THAN A CONQUEROR** means that ALL BELIEVERS can pray in one city and God will send the answer or solve the problem instantly thousands of miles away.

Always remember that all things are indeed working for the good of ALL BELIEVERS (Ro. 8:28) and that no weapon or strategy that is formed against God's servants will prosper (Is. 54:17).

"...Giving thanks unto the Father, which hath made us met to be partakers of the inheritance of the saints in light: Who hath delivered us from the power of darkness, and hath translated us into the kingdom of his dear Son." (Col. 1:12, 13)

"And NOW, brethren, I commend you to God, and to the WORD OF HIS GRACE, WHICH IS ABLE TO BUILD YOU UP, and to give you an inheritance among ALL THEM which are sanctified." (Acts 20:32)

Let us hear the CONCLUSION OF THE WHOLE MATTER.

MUCH PRAYER — MUCH POWER[60]

LITTLE PRAYER — LITTLE POWER

No prayer — no power

*Of self — NONE **OF GOD***

*Less of self — MORE **OF GOD***

NONE OF SELF — ALL OF GOD

---

60   A quote from Wigglesworth Smith, a 20th century evangelist.

Being a warrior is not an option.

It is a mandate straight from the Throne Room!

"But thanks be to God who giveth us the victory through our Lord and Savior, Jesus Christ. Therefore, my beloved brethren, be ye stedfast, unmoveable, always abounding in the work of the Lord, forasmuch as ye know that your labor is not in vain in the Lord." **(I Corinthians 15:57, 58).**

APPENDIX 1

THE NAMES OF SATAN

Satan (I Thess. 2:18)

"Satan" means "adversary," "opposer." If he wanted to mount the throne of God, it should not be too difficult to understand that he is so full of hate toward God and all men that he will do anything and everything to also oppose God's will for man.

The Devil (Rev. 12:9)

From the Greek word "diabolos," "devil" means "slanderer," "malignant accuser." Notice that "devil" is always used with "the" to indicate the highly specialized, perfected ability to accuse day and night.[61]

Beelzebub (Matt. 12:24,27)

Even though Beelzebub in Matthew 12:24 was called the "prince of devils," the name is translated "lord of flies," which means "one with genius to cause corruption." Everyone has

---

61   See Job, Chapters 1, 2 and Rev. 12:10.

observed the proliferation of flies and maggots around filth, whether it's garbage, animal or human excreta, or dead flesh. Flies touch and eat filth, vomit and eat the filth again; then, the filth is passed to another object as the flies travels. Satan (Beelzebub) defiles and corrupts everything, whether it is governments (Iran-Contra or Watergate scandals), economics (the Savings and Loan debacle), families (with substance abuse, incest, violence, and divorce), etc.

The Serpent (Rev. 12:9)

Satan as the serpent is sly, subtle, cunning, wise, and treacherous; in other words, the epitome of deceit and hypocrisy. Remember, the serpent deceived Eve by his craftiness (II Cor. 11:3). Lucifer's God-given wisdom degenerated into Satan's serpentine craftiness and evil cunning—unexpected malignant events.

The Prince of the Power of the Air (Eph. 2:2)

Satan was defeated, ejected, dispossessed, and thrown out of the Mount of God somewhere in the heavens. He does operate in the atmosphere, above the earth. Satan is temporary tenant of the air and atmosphere in homes, buildings, your neighborhood, your schools, and any place that has not been dedicated to God and where no prayer exists. Through the myriad of demons manipulating and managing ambiance, he can cause riots, gang rapes, unexpected rage, etc.

Murderer (John 8:44)

Although a murderer, in the absolute sense of the word, is

one who takes the life of another, permutations of murder include, but are not limited to, character assassination, the devastation of churches through strife and divisiveness, and hatred. Notice that John 10:10 informs us that the thief (Satan) comes only to <u>kill</u>, <u>steal</u>, and <u>destroy</u>.

The Roaring Lion (I Peter 5:8)

A lion watches, stalks, waits until his prey is most vulnerable, attacks, and then can successfully devour. Once a lion attacks, he continues to devour until nothing is remaining of the prey. Further, you will never know a lion's intentions, location, or time of the strike.

Liar (John 8:44)

A lie is something told or done with the intent to deceive. Therefore, Satan will use even truth to deceive. For example, persons with religious demons can and do preach some truth. Spiritualist churches as well as many cults preach some truth. Bear in mind that Satan is the father of all lies, using trickery and deceit to skillfully deceive (even perhaps the very elect).

The Tempter (Matt. 4:3)

"Tempt" refers to "inciting to do evil" and failing in commitments and obedience. The skillfulness of Satan is that he does not allow himself to be identified as engineering and orchestrating the temptations. (Note that God can allow temptations to be tests and trials—stepping stones to God's greatness.)

The Dragon (Rev. 12:3)

The dragon as used in Revelations refers to an awesome, powerful monster that will still be trying to ferociously exercise malignant force and power in the "end of time."

The Evil One (I John 5:19)

Satan personifies absolute evil—therefore, the use of the definite article "the" before "evil." Just as God is Love without any qualifying statement, Satan is <u>evil</u>. Language and other forms of communication are a marvelous gift from God. However, we become prisoners of the limitation of language when there is an attempt to explain the abhorrent, grotesque evil of Satan. He cannot win The War, but he can win YOU if you fall short of God's will and command.

The Accuser of the Brethren (Rev. 12:10)

Satan will accuse, criticize, lie about you to yourself (guilt and condemnation), to God (Rev. 12:10), and to your family and friends. Notice that in his nature as an accuser, he will even use the truth when it suits him.

APPENDIX II

The Acts Of The Sinful Nature

(Galatians 5:19, 20)

SEXUAL IMMORALITY: (From the Greek word *porneia*) Referring to all immoral sexual conduct including ALL sexual intercourse out of the marital bonds; fornication, adultery, homosexuality, incest, pedophilia, and polluted sexual acts between husband wife like anal sex. Watching X-rated movies, reading polluted writings, and indulging in looking at pornographic pictures are included. Feeling on another person who is not your spouse is an immoral sexual act.

IMPURITY: (From the Greek word *akatharsia)* Includes all sexual sins, evils deeds and vices, and wicked, ungodly thoughts (including lusting after a man or woman) and desires.

DEBAUCHERY: (From the Greek word *aselgeia)* Refers to excessively indulging one's passions and desires without any shame or public decency; sensuality.

IDOLATRY: (From the Greek word *eidololatria*) Means the worship of spirits, persons, or graven images; giving greater allegiance and commitment to any person, institution, or thing than to the authority of God and the Word of God. (Sometimes we make idols of our children, our possessions, and dressing, even our leaders.)

WITCHCRAFT: (From the Greek word *pharmakeia*) This encompasses sorcery, spiritism, black magic, worship of demons, use of drugs (producing mind-altered states and/or a passive mind); any kind of mind control, in order to have a person and their behavior dominated by Satan and his demons.

HATRED: (From the Greek word *echthra*) This means malicious dislike or enmity; intense hostile intentions and acts.

DISCORD: (From the Greek word *eris)* This refers to quarreling, antagonism, conflict, disagreement, strife; a struggle for superiority.

JEALOUSY: (From the Greek word *zelos)* Resentfulness, envy of another's success, looks, and/or possessions.

FITS OF RAGE: (Greek word *thumos*) Uncontrollable anger with destructive behavior and words.

SELFISH AMBITION: (Greek word *eritheia*) Seeking power, money, fame, and favor for personal reasons.

DISSENSIONS: (Greek word *dichostasia)* Introducing divisive teachings not supported by God's Word or openly and verbally opposing teaching and leadership in the church.

FACTIONS: (From the Greek word *hairesis*) Divisions within the congregation into clubs and elite cliques that destroy the unity of the church.

ENVY: (From the Greek word *phthonos*) Resentful and disliking a person for having something that one desires.

DRUNKENNESS: (From the Greek word *methe*) Impairing one's thinking ability and body by too much alcoholic drink.

ORGIES: (From the Greek word *komos*) Excesses in feasting and revelry, generally involving alcohol, drugs, sex, and the like.

Compare Colossians 3:5-8, which includes a similar list of all the evil that must be *put to death*.

In July of 2012, on a mission trip to Australia, the church and its grounds were so polluted, we, in conjunction with the pastor, cleansed the property by taking each one of the above and we bound, rebuked, dispossessed, and cast them out and off the church grounds. We then loosed to take up residence all the manifestations of the "Fruit of the Spirit" (Gal. 5:22).

APPENDIX III

SCRIPTURE MEMORIZATION

You need to plan how you are going to continuously memorize scripture. The basics to any Bible memory plan are as follows:

1. **Develop a system for the areas to be memorized.** For example, you should begin with scriptures that give reasons to memorize scripture: Psalm 119:11, 105, Col. 3:16. Or, warfare scriptures: Luke 10:19, James 4:7, Matt. 16:19, I John 4:4; Rev. 12:11. Or healing scriptures: Isaiah 53:5, Matt. 8:17, I Peter 2:24; Psalms 100:3.

2. **Develop a method.** For example, write the scriptures to be memorized on three-by-five cards. Place them your bag, briefcase, or pocket of your car. When you have spare time, take them out and study them. At home, place the scripture that you are currently memorizing over the sink in the kitchen, or over the bathroom sink. Review and memorize. Memorize and review. Sometimes writing and rewriting the

same scripture over and over is helpful.

3. **Whenever you hear a message that is particularly meaningful to you or that does something special for you, take the text of the message and memorize it.** These are the easiest scriptures to memorize because the message is already in your heart.

4. **When Satan is tormenting your mind, discipline your mind by learning more scriptures.** Challenge yourself to learn the entire 27th Psalm or the entire 8th chapter of Romans.

5. At the beginning of weekly Bible study, you can ask the pastor to allow you to have a Bible memory course conducted. It is easier to memorize scripture when you work at it with others.

DEVOTIONAL BIBLE READING

Devotional Bible reading is that period of time every day during which you fellowship with God and listen to Him. Not only do you pray and meditate, but you must be consistent and dedicated to hearing from God. One of the ways is with your daily devotions—READING THE WORD OF GOD. Notice that discipline is easiest with a pattern. Pick the same time each day (if possible) and the same spot (if possible).

Recommendations

1. Read at least **one chapter in Proverbs daily**.

Proverbs helps you in your relationships with others as well as with God. (John Wesley, Billy Graham, and many other great men of God stated that they always read some in Proverbs and the Psalms daily). **Read at least five chapters in Psalms** daily. Help train your mind into praise and prayer. Since the 119th Psalm is so lengthy, read it in two days.

2. **The Sermon on the Mount, Matthew 5, 6, 7, should be read from time to time.** Jesus proclaims His beliefs toward law, position, authority, and money. He essentially teaches in these scriptures that the most important issue is faithful and absolute obedience to God.

3. **Read regularly John 14, 15, 16;** Jesus teaching about the Holy Spirit.

4. **Read regularly Acts 1, 2, 3;** the powerful beginning of the Christian church.

5. **Read regularly I Corinthians 12, 13, 14.** Chapter 12 explains the Gifts. Chapter 13 explains the essence of Love that is of God. Chapter 14 explains spiritual Gifts, particularly "tongues."

6. **Ephesians 1 and 6 and Romans 8** deal with the believer's "battle lines" and preparation for battle.

7. **Genesis and the Gospel of John** are two books all new Christians should become familiar with.

BIBLIOGRAPHY

The Holy Bible, King James Version

The Holy Bible, New International Version (NIV)

The Holy Bible, Revised Standard Version

Fay Ellis Butler, *Called to Be Saints*

Rejection, The Ruling Spirit

After Deliverance, Then What?

Charles Finney, *Revivals of Religion*

Lowell Hart, *Satan's Music Exposed*

Dave Hunt & T.A. McMahon, *The Seduction of Christianity*

Johanna Michaelson, *The Lambs to the Slaughter*

Watchman Nee, *The Latent Power of the Soul*

The Spiritual Man

Even So, Come Lord Jesus

Rick Renner, *Dressed to Kill*

William Schnoebelen, *Masonry, Beyond the Light*

Merrill F. Unger, *Demons in the World Today*

Vine's **Expository Dictionary of Bible Words**

OTHER BOOKS
BY THE AUTHOR

CALLED TO BE SAINTS. This book, with Biblical support, teaches, step by step, strategies to defeat the enemy of your mind, how to be healed of the painful past, and how to take personal responsibility for your personal growth. **$10.00**

AFTER DELIVERANCE, THEN WHAT? Satan never stops! Even after your deliverance, he will attempt to oppress you with the same "unclean spirits" and/or your past. You are only "more than a conqueror" if you understand the warfare and fight. **$5.00**

HOW TO MINISTER TO CHRISTIANS IN BONDAGE. This work will open up your understanding to the way Satan attacks the mind, spirit, and body. The book will enable the reader to recognize and deal with the spirits of oppression and depression; how to be delivered from bondage; and ways to avoid bondage. **$5.00**

REJECTION, THE RULING SPIRIT. Read to learn how "ruling spirits" manifest themselves in our personal and spiritual lives, and how Satan uses them to magnify feelings of inferiority, defeat, and worthlessness. **$15.00**

SEXUAL ABUSE, PAIN, DELIVERANCE. Deals with the pain, guilt, and horror of incest, rape, and fondling (of males and females). This work gives an overview of the problem, explaining what takes place mentally and spiritually when the victim is abused—how some demonic transference occurs. Focuses on the pain of betrayal by caregivers and family members and finally on the healing process. **$15.00**

THE HOLY SPIRIT; DON'T LIVE HERE OR LEAVE HERE WITHOUT HIM. Deals with the executive Head of the Trinity operating in and through the believer. Discusses why being filled and refilled regularly is necessary for living and warring against the enemy. **$10.00**

THE IGNORANCE CRISIS. Explores question like "What happened to the fire of the Holy Ghost?", "What happened to the keys to the kingdom?" and other important issues. ***The Seduction of the Saints*** is no longer in print because it has been included in this book. **$12.00**

WHY ARE GOD'S PEOPLE SICK? Find out why believers are taking just as much medicine as unbelievers and visiting the doctor just as much as those who do not profess salvation. The author addresses the issues of not adhering to I Peter 5:7 and Philippians 4:6. **$5.00**

WHY PRAY? Focuses on the reasons for constant prayer, the types of prayer, the persistence and results of prayer, and particularly the things the Lord instructed about prayer. **$5.00.**

Check Yourself, Rights, Rewards, and Responsibilities, How to Know the Will of God for Your Life has been incorporated in *CALLED TO BE SAINTS*. *Seduction of the Saints* has been included in *THE IGNORANCE CRISIS*.

TO ORDER

ADD 15% FOR POSTAGE AND HANDLING

MAIL CHECK OR MONEY ORDER PAYABLE TO:

Dr. Fay Ellis Butler

P.O. Box 330995, Stuyvesant Station

Brooklyn, New York 11233